American Business History: A Very Short Introduction

VERY SHORT INTRODUCTIONS are for anyone wanting a stimulating and accessible way into a new subject. They are written by experts, and have been translated into more than 45 different languages.

The series began in 1995, and now covers a wide variety of topics in every discipline. The VSI library currently contains over 600 volumes—a Very Short Introduction to everything from Psychology and Philosophy of Science to American History and Relativity—and continues to grow in every subject area.

Very Short Introductions available now:

Available soon:

For more information visit our web site
www.oup.com/vsi/

Walter A. Friedman

AMERICAN
BUSINESS
HISTORY

A Very Short Introduction

OXFORD
UNIVERSITY PRESS

OXFORD
UNIVERSITY PRESS

Oxford University Press is a department of the University of Oxford.
It furthers the University's objective of excellence in research, scholarship,
and education by publishing worldwide. Oxford is a registered trade mark of
Oxford University Press in the UK and certain other countries.

Published in the United States of America by Oxford University Press
198 Madison Avenue, New York, NY 10016, United States of America.

Library of Congress Control Number: 2020935562

ISBN 978-0-19-062247-3

Printed by Integrated Books International, United States of America
on acid-free paper

For you, Orli

Acknowledgments

I would like to thank Rachael Comunale and Kristine Haglund for their help and advice throughout this project and Nancy Toff, at Oxford University Press, for suggesting the topic in the first place. I appreciate the support of Harvard Business School, especially that of Dean Nitin Nohria, the Division of Research and Faculty Development, and Baker Library. I would also like to thank those who made suggestions along the way, including Sven Beckert, Leslie Berlin, Brian Cheffins, James Cortada, Peter Eisenstadt, Jeanette Estruth, David Frankel, Robert Fredona, Marc and Danielle Green, Per Hansen, Richard R. John, Ana Kolendo, Laura Linard, David Moss, Tom Nicholas, Rowena Olegario, Natasha Overmeyer, Susie Pak, Larry Perlov, Jennifer Quick, Sophus Reinert, Christine Riggle, Laura Phillips Sawyer, Nitzan Shear, Jonathan Silvers, Jeff Strabone, Richard Tedlow, Charles Wilson, Mark Wilson, and Robert Wright. I am especially grateful to my family, Susan Burgin and Orli Friedman.

Contents

List of illustrations

Introduction: A business civilization

The thought of the United States becoming the world's richest and most powerful nation would have been unimaginable at the time of the country's founding. In 1783, at the end of the American Revolution, the United States was a marginal commercial center, far from the powers of Europe and the riches of Asia. It was a farm-based, subsistence economy with a small export trade in grains, tobacco, and salted fish and limited manufacturing.

In 1800, the US census, which excluded Native Americans, counted the population at 5.3 million people, about 17 percent of whom were enslaved. The population was significantly smaller than that of Great Britain, which stood at about 10.5 million people, and that of France, with 26.8 million, let alone China, the most populous nation, with 300 million.

In the nineteenth century, the United States, like several European countries, experienced unprecedented economic growth and a rise in per capita income. In terms of wealth, in 1820, the gross domestic product per capita of the United States was just below that of Italy and the Netherlands and about two-thirds that of Great Britain. Much of the rise in aggregate and per capita wealth in the United States, in the decades after independence until the Civil War, came from a growing manufacturing sector, especially in textiles; a rising international trade in commodities such as whale oil; and improvements in the enlistment of new energy sources, especially coal, and advancements in transportation in the form of canals and railroads. It rested, too, through the mid-1860s, on a cruel and brutal slave-based plantation system in the South producing raw cotton for the global economy.

In the late nineteenth century, the United States outpaced its European rivals in rate of population growth, industrial output, and agriculture. A major factor spurring this rise in wealth was the continued growth of business enterprise and the government policies that enabled its unprecedented scale and scope. Entrepreneurs and innovators improved methods of transportation, completing transcontinental railroads and transatlantic telegraph cables. Some built vast trading networks—warehousing, packaging, and distributing the country's agricultural resources. Others created massive factories churning out oil, steel, chemicals, and complex machinery like reapers, cash registers, and electrical motors. Still others built vital financial enterprises, supplied credit, made investments, and floated securities. By 1913, the United States was the world's largest producer of both manufactured goods and agricultural products. Moreover, the size of the country's largest firms—which by then had as many as several thousand employees—meant that managerial and executive decision-making impacted not only the firm itself but also, in some instances, national economic achievements and trajectories.

Yet the growth of business in America was neither automatic nor predetermined. The idea that business would come to shape so much of American life, altering the very landscape and skyline of the country, would not have occurred to the nation's founders. Nor would Adam Smith, who penned his classic economic treatise, *The Wealth of Nations*, in 1776, have predicted the rise of business in such a spectacular fashion. In Smith's time, businesses shared none of the characteristics of modern enterprise—no separation of ownership and management, no professional managers, and no corporate bureaucracies. Smith could hardly have foreseen the development of a large, complex corporation like General Motors, which by 1955 had 624,000 employees around the world.

By the early twentieth century, the United States was frequently described as having a culture dominated by business. In 1929, Pulitzer Prize–winning historian James Truslow Adams published *Our Business Civilization*, which conveyed the extent to which business had permeated American society. In America, Adams wrote, "unlike Europe, the business man . . . finds himself the dominant power in the life of the nation and almost alone in his control over the direction of its entire life, economic, social, intellectual, religious, and political." He added, "It is a situation that, so far as I know, is unique in history."

More recently, the historian Sven Beckert likened iconic classical architecture to the extensive commercial and industrial infrastructure that spread across the United States during the nineteenth and twentieth centuries: "While Athens had its Parthenon and Rome its Colosseum, the United States had its River Rouge Factory in Detroit [and] the stockyards of Chicago." In each case, these structures seemed to somehow capture the essence of these societies.

But how did business organizations gain such a central place in American society? What was it about the United States that made the country so alluring to entrepreneurs, both foreign and domestic? How did the United States come to have the largest business enterprises in the world by the early twentieth century? Moreover, what was the nature of a society in which businesspeople played such a leading role—not just in economic affairs, but also in politics and culture?

In answering these questions, this book emphasizes several overlapping themes: a capitalist orientation in policymaking that, while at times varying in the extent of government regulation and intervention in the economy, generally favored economic growth; a spirit of democratic entrepreneurship that encouraged people, both domestically and from around the world, to found businesses in the United States; an approach to management that embraced innovation and pursued operation at immense scale; and a financial system that, through investment banks, venture capital firms, and other institutions, enabled the commercialization of new technologies and ideas. All four themes, sometimes in concert with each other and other times in conflict, help explain the growth and trajectory of American enterprise to the present day.

Chapter 1
Trade and empire

By the late fifteenth century there are estimated to have been between 50 and 100 million people living in the Americas, about 5 to 10 million of whom were located in the present-day United States and Canada. These indigenous Americans had developed, over centuries, complex social and economic systems that governed tribal relationships across vast spaces. The arrival of Europeans seeking to find trade routes, colonize, and in other ways gain wealth from these lands disrupted and devastated the balance of life that had existed for millennia.

After Christopher Columbus's first landing in the Caribbean in 1492, the Spanish built an empire that, at its height, stretched from present-day Florida and California to Tierra del Fuego in Argentina. In the 1540s, the discovery of silver deposits in modern-day Mexico and Bolivia led to the establishment of vast mining operations that enriched the Spanish Crown with bullion. The sheer amount of silver carted across the ocean brought a surge of wealth to Spanish royalty and ignited interest in the New World. By 1565, the Spanish had established the first surviving settlement in what would become the United States, St. Augustine (in present-day Florida), which was just one point of many in their New World empire.

In the 1530s, French explorers built settlements along the northeast coast of North America, in present-day Canada, and later developed trade routes deep into the interior, along the St. Lawrence River in the north and down the Mississippi River. This region, though it lacked gold and other precious metals found farther south, was rich in valuable animal furs, which could be sent back to Europe for a handsome profit.

The English were relative latecomers in the colonization of the Americas. One of the earliest ventures was the settlement of a colony in present-day North Carolina, at Roanoke, in 1585. The venture failed after only a few years, but other English settlements in the region followed, most notably Jamestown in 1607. Farther north, a group of English settlers founded the Massachusetts Bay Colony in 1628. In 1664, the English took control over the Dutch settlements in New Amsterdam, at the tip of Manhattan, renaming the area New York.

The growth of the Spanish, French, and English (after 1707, British) commercial empires was predicated on the seizure of land and resources from the native peoples who were living across North and South America. However, the nature of European interactions with native peoples varied significantly. In Spanish Mexico, colonizers practiced a policy of subjugation—through violent force and missionary zeal—to eventually establish a dominant relationship over nearby tribes, including the Pueblos, Apalachee, Apache, and Ute. In this way, the Spanish maintained control over the region's productive gold and silver mines. To the north, the French were much more dependent on the knowledge and skill of native peoples to extract the most precious resources— animal furs. As a result, they frequently entered alliances with different tribes, including the Montagnais, Algonquin, Huron, and, later, the Haudenosaunee Five Nations (or Iroquois), to trade European manufactured goods for otter, fox, beaver, and lynx furs. English colonists to the south were in a unique position—at once dependent on the knowledge of native tribes to survive and bent on seizing land for agriculture and eradicating Indian customs.

European domination over Native Americans was never a foregone conclusion. However, one factor—disease—radically altered North American demographics, and thus the balance of power between tribes and colonizers, in the centuries after initial contact. Europeans introduced many new diseases including smallpox, cholera, and bubonic plague, to which North American tribes had no immunity. By 1700, as a result of the outbreak of major epidemics, native populations stood at just one-tenth of precontact numbers. The decline in Native American populations was so rapid that, until 1776, there was a net population loss in North America, even with the new European arrivals. By 1800, roughly only 600,000 Native Americans remained in the United States and Canada. At the same time, the United States had a total population of about 5.3 million, including 900,000 enslaved persons.

Founding companies

In the most direct sense, the early English trading companies that colonized North America planted the seeds of American business. The distinct nature of the economies that evolved in each of the different English colonies worked in unexpected yet complementary ways to create a robust network of Atlantic trade.

After the doomed effort at Roanoke, English investors and colonizers organized settlements in North America as joint-stock companies—a significant innovation that allowed a larger number of investors to share both risk and reward. England became a pioneer in joint-stock enterprises, to which the Crown granted rights to trade in specific regions of the globe. Some were large and lasted centuries, like the East India Company (founded 1600), which came to control much of the Indian subcontinent. Others were smaller, like the Muscovy Company (1551), which failed in its aim to explore the Northwest Passage, but temporarily established trade relations with Moscow. The Hudson Bay Company, established in 1670, entered the fur trade and is still in operation in the early twenty-first century (as a Canadian retail group). These chartered companies are some of the first familiar names that we recognize today as *businesses*.

Two of the most significant joint-stock companies established during this period were the Virginia Company (founded 1606) and the Massachusetts Bay Company (1628), which settled the colonies of Jamestown and Massachusetts Bay, respectively. Many of the early Jamestown settlers perished in the first few years after arrival, but a new supply of provisions and colonists reached Virginia in 1609, allowing the colony to survive. Jamestown continued to grow under the management of Sir Edwin Sandys, Earl of Southampton, who promised voyagers grants of land and also endorsed a system of indentured servitude to attract the young, who otherwise did not have the means to travel to the colony.

But it was the cultivation of tobacco, starting around 1612, that ensured the colony's survival. Colonists exported most of the crop to England, where demand grew steadily. In 1615 and 1616, Virginia exported 2,300 pounds of tobacco. By 1617, that number had increased nearly tenfold to 20,000 pounds. With dwindling Native American populations and a drop in indentured servitude, tobacco growers turned to a brutal alternative: the growing transatlantic slave trade. In 1619, Dutch traders brought the first documented slaves from Africa to Jamestown, Virginia. By the mid-seventeenth century, enslaved labor became an ingrained part of the Southern agricultural system.

The Massachusetts Bay Colony was very different—in terms of both economy and demography—from its southern neighbor. The settlement grew in size after an influx of Puritans from England in the 1620s and especially the 1630s, during the period known as

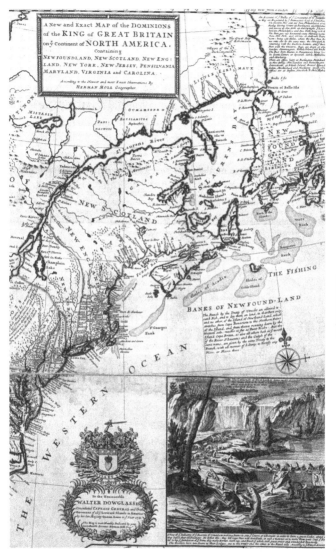

1. Herman Moll, Thomas Bowles, and John Bowles, *A New and Exact Map of the Dominions of the King of Great Britain on ye Continent of North America* (section), ca. 1732. In addition to showing purely geographical features, the map depicts the rich resources of the land; the inset shows a flourishing family of beavers.

the *Great Migration*. However, when immigration rates began to fall in the 1640s, so too did the frequency of incoming supply ships. Colonists needed to find other ways to survive, and the rocky soil and short growing season meant that they could not rely on a lucrative cash crop, as colonists in Virginia could. Instead, they pursued trade in furs and salted fish and capitalized on the ready availability of timber to build ships to take their goods to market. Indeed, shipbuilding became a thriving industry in Massachusetts during this period and connected the colony with other English settlements along the Atlantic coast, in particular the West Indies sugar islands. Salted fish from New England helped to grow the sugar industry on islands like Barbados (and later Jamaica) by feeding the large enslaved workforce. In this way, albeit indirectly, the Massachusetts economy was also intimately linked to the slave trade.

The economies that developed in the English colonies of Jamestown and Massachusetts Bay thus looked very different from the purely extractive economies that emerged in the Spanish and French colonies to the south and north. From very early on, they became deeply involved in the more extensive network of English transatlantic trade and commerce and helped to establish England (later, Britain) as the dominant European force in North America.

Indeed, over time, eleven other colonies joined Massachusetts and Virginia: New Hampshire (1629), Maryland (1632), Connecticut (1636), Rhode Island (1636), New York (1664), Delaware (1664), New Jersey (1664), Pennsylvania (1681), North and South Carolina (1712), and Georgia (1732). In addition to Virginia, the Carolinas, Maryland, and even Pennsylvania contributed to agricultural production, specializing in the cultivation of tobacco and rice. Because of the widespread availability of land, roughly 80 percent of colonists were subsistence farmers during the colonial period.

From 1763 (the year that marked the end of the Seven Years' War between Britain and France) to the start of the American Revolution in 1775, some 221,500 people came to the British colonies in North America. Many were Europeans, whose migration was driven by circumstance and ambition. This group included 55,000 Protestant Irish, 40,000 Scots, and 30,000 English. Some 12,000 German-speaking immigrants arrived in Philadelphia. However, many more arrivals, some 84,500, were enslaved Africans taken from their homes by violence. The result was a diverse population drawn from many localities, speaking many languages, possessing different customs and traditions, coming by choice or by force, and practicing a wide range of trades and crafts that helped to build the nascent colonial economy.

Merchants

In the 1770s, the largest cities in British North America were Philadelphia (population approximately 28,000) and New York (25,000), followed by Boston (16,000); Charleston, South Carolina (12,000); and Newport, Rhode Island (11,000). In these thriving ports arose a new merchant elite, among them the Brown family of Providence, Rhode Island, and the Carrolls and the Ridgelys of Maryland. Elias Hasket Derby from Salem, Massachusetts, pioneered trade directly with China in the 1780s and became one of the wealthiest men in New England.

Indeed, merchants became leading figures in the colonial economy—importers and exporters, bankers and insurers, retailers and wholesalers. They lent money to planters and artisans and, with other merchants, arranged for the shipping of goods. When necessary, they insured ships and cargoes and built piers and ports. They also created distilleries and shipyards and sent family members to London, the West Indies, and other international cities to serve as overseas agents.

Thomas Hancock was one such merchant. Hancock began his commercial life by opening a bookshop, the Bible & Three Crowns, in the North End of Boston. He became a partner in a paper mill and began to import British manufactured goods, exporting codfish, whale oil, and potash. He soon expanded into other business ventures, quickly making the Hancock family one of the wealthiest and most prominent in Boston. Thomas's nephew, John Hancock—best known for his oversized signature on the Declaration of Independence—became involved in the family business and traveled to Great Britain to acquaint himself with customers and suppliers. When he took over Hancock Manor, it was considered among the most elegant houses in the colonies. Situated near the Boston Common, it included several buildings and depended on the work of several enslaved persons who ran the orchard and the household.

General merchants, like the Hancock family, typically owned their ships and conducted trade around the world in a variety of goods. They operated throughout the Atlantic, the West Indies, and the Iberian Peninsula—importing manufactured goods, rum, sugar, wine, lemons, and more—while engaging in export trade in meat, flour, lumber, and flaxseed. Rural storeowners purchased imports on credit or sometimes paid merchants in the form of commodities (including tobacco, rice, and sugar in the South and furs, pelts, and wampum shells in the North), bills of exchange, or sterling. Because of the undeveloped market and lack of commercial infrastructure to transport goods into the interior, store owners often picked up their goods directly at the pier. A leading merchant had few employees but would typically hire a watchman to safeguard merchandise, a clerk to keep correspondence, and a bookkeeper to track transactions.

Colonies and metropole

For much of the seventeenth and eighteenth centuries, the British colonies in North America existed in an interdependent, yet largely unregulated, relationship with Britain in a period known as *salutary neglect*. The colonies provided raw materials for British manufacturing and themselves consumed a large percentage of resultant British finished goods. During this period, the English and then British governments made several attempts to implement stricter mercantile regulation. The passage of the Navigation Acts, a series of laws beginning in 1651, for example, was intended to restrict colonial trade with other countries and simultaneously stem colonial manufacturing. However, in practice, these rules were poorly enforced and often subverted by piracy and smuggling.

The period of salutary neglect came to an end in the early 1760s. Britain, struggling with significant debt incurred during the Seven Years' War with France, began to impose and enforce colonial taxes and tariffs. These included the Stamp Act (1765), the Townshend Acts (1767 and 1768), and later a collection of legislation known as the Coercive Acts—enacted in response to the 1773 Boston Tea Party, when American Sons of Liberty, an organization of revolutionaries, dumped tea from the East India Company into the harbor. Though the size of tariffs was minimal compared to those imposed on the British taxpayer, the sudden change in British policy concerning the colonies triggered a prolonged and heated debate over the questions of taxation and representation.

The way to wealth

The thriving colonial printing industry gave voice to political debates. In the 1760s and early 1770s, many newspapers took sides in the intensifying quarrels between loyalists and patriots over the question of independence from Britain. Some, like the *Virginia Gazette*, became advocates of the patriot cause. Others, like the *Boston Post-Boy*, remained loyal to the Crown. Printers also published broadsides and pamphlets that championed independence, including Thomas Paine's *Common Sense*, published in Philadelphia in 1776.

One of the most popular pieces of writing published during this time, however, was interested not in the question of political independence from Great Britain, but in a subject that became an American standard: how to achieve prosperity. Benjamin Franklin's essay *The Way to Wealth* first appeared in 1758 under a different name; its now-famous title was adopted only in 1773. The book was not original in its sentiments, but it distilled, refined, and popularized a series of ideas that countered millennia-old proscriptions against wealth seeking. Indeed, in *The Way to Wealth*, Franklin explained how learning a trade and working hard at it could lead an individual out of poverty, while also contributing to the economic health of the country. "In short, the way to wealth, if you desire it, is as plain as the way to market," wrote Franklin: "It depends chiefly on two words: industry and frugality." He detested wastefulness and sloth. "Remember that time is money," Franklin advised. He championed the role of the craftsman within a larger world of mercantile trade and argued that business enterprise could offer a path to social mobility and self-determination—essential elements of what, much later, became known as the *American Dream*. (The phrase was first coined by historian James Truslow Adams in the early twentieth century to describe the aspiration of "a better, richer, and happier life for all our citizens of every rank.")

By 1850, *The Way to Wealth* had been published in a remarkable 1,100 editions worldwide. It was one of the best-selling books of the period and by far the most popular source of personal and economic advice. Franklin's book was an economic and social declaration of independence, in many ways akin to the political Declaration of Independence of 1776, and one that had an enduring place in the American conception of business activity.

Chapter 2
Commerce in the new nation, 1780–1820

In the decades after the American Revolution, from 1790 (the first US census) to 1820, the US population grew from 3.9 million to 9.6 million. In 1803, the country effectively doubled in size following the Louisiana Purchase, the acquisition of land from France that included territory west of the Mississippi River to the Rocky Mountains. Farming and agriculture continued to be the most common occupations. In 1800, 83 percent of the workforce labored in these industries.

Yet other types of business activity, including manufacturing, also began to grow during this period, in some cases roughly following the pattern of development described by the Scottish political theorist Adam Smith. In *Inquiry into the Nature and Causes of the Wealth of Nations* (1776), Smith argued that increased output came from the division of labor in manufactures and the specialization of trade. Sure enough, in the years after the American Revolution, as the pace of business increased, the general merchants who had dominated the colonial economy increasingly found themselves in competition with more specialized merchants, who traded only in certain commodities, like cotton, fur and pelts, lumber, sugar, tobacco, and whale oil, or who carried out a specific business function, like warehousing or insuring.

However, the national economy got off to a rocky start. Immediately after the end of the Revolutionary War, the nation fell into a deep recession—one that some economists see as nearly as severe as the Great Depression of the 1930s. During the war, Congress had accumulated a debt of $27 million, owed to Continental soldiers for their service during the war, to farmers who sold goods and supplies to the Continental Army, and to foreign creditors who had supported the American cause. Congress, as outlined in the Articles of Confederation (ratified in 1781), was unable to levy taxes and thus unable to pay this debt. The Articles of Confederation had largely preserved the sovereignty of each state and provided little power to the federal government.

It was not until 1788, with the ratification of the Constitution, that the contours of the American republic began to take shape, with its characteristic distribution of power among the three branches of government (executive, legislative, and judicial), as well as between the federal and state governments. Indeed, federalism became a defining characteristic of the US government, ensuring that, at least in this period, corporations would have state charters rather than national ones.

The Constitution also helped to foster domestic industry by allowing for tariffs on imports, forbidding taxes on goods sold across states (which was essential for the creation of a large domestic market), and, importantly, prohibiting states from passing laws to "impair the obligation of contracts," a necessary legal step for the development of business.

Alexander Hamilton was a key figure in the development of early American economic policy. Hamilton was born on the Caribbean island of Nevis and worked for a merchant trading firm as a teenager before arriving in New York City. This early experience gave him a unique perspective on the problems facing a debt-ridden country with an agricultural population. He served as the first secretary of the Treasury (1789–95) and during that time made several significant contributions to securing the commercial and financial foundations of the American economy. In 1790, he promoted a controversial plan to have the national government assume states' war debts—a move that would reassure European creditors of the financial soundness of the new nation, yet also reward speculators for buying up debt at prices far below face value. The proposal passed, but only after a compromise with Southern congressmen that moved the new US capital from New York City to Washington, DC.

The following year, Hamilton published his *Report on Manufactures* (1791), which called for federal support of industry and manufacturing. He proposed several possible ways to achieve strong economic growth, for instance, by providing subsidies for industry and imposing tariffs on imported goods and by the implementation of production bounties, as a way to keep prices up. Hamilton also pushed for the creation of a central bank, which was realized with the founding of the Bank of the United States (chartered from 1791 to 1811). These measures, Hamilton believed, would help the United States protect and defend itself in times of war.

The rise of business in the decades immediately following the Revolution was also aided by a commercial culture that attracted immigrant entrepreneurs. Éleuthère Irénée du Pont, for example, fled his native France in 1800, bringing with him a knowledge of chemistry. Shortly after his arrival in the United States, he opened an explosives manufactory on the Brandywine Creek near Wilmington, Delaware, and imported machinery from France. E. I. du Pont de Nemours & Company became one of the country's largest suppliers of gunpowder.

The contours of modern unions also began to take shape during the early republic period. Although European guild-style associations never took hold to the same degree in the American colonies, there were comparable trade associations, particularly among carpenters, shoemakers (cordwainers), tailors, and printers. Philadelphia printers undertook one of the first recorded strikes in 1786, successfully lobbying for higher wages of six dollars per week.

Roads and canals

One aspect of trade that improved markedly during the early republic period was the ability to transport and distribute goods. American merchants continued to expand the reach of their overseas shipping, sending ships regularly to China and other far-flung places. Importantly, the delivery of goods, whether domestic or imported, to the interior of the United States began to become easier. Beginning in the late 1790s, many new corporations (often in the form of joint-stock companies) emerged, seeking to improve domestic trade by building roads. In 1795, the Lancaster Turnpike Company linked Philadelphia with Lancaster, Pennsylvania, about seventy miles to the west.

Canals allowed for a substantial increase in the weight horses could pull on riverbanks and augmented the network of rivers to reach the interior of the country. The most important canal project was the 360-mile Erie Canal, completed in 1825. The canal allowed for lower shipping costs and greater speed. A flatboat loaded with cargo at Lake Erie in Buffalo, New York, could travel to Albany and down the Hudson River to New York City's Atlantic port in just six days, and, conversely, imported goods—for instance, dry goods from Manchester, iron from Sweden, and tea from China—could easily reach the interior after originally landing on Manhattan's docks. New transportation technologies, most significantly the steamboat, also facilitated distribution.

The steamboat substantially improved the pace and reliability of transportation. Like many important inventions of the day (including the spinning jenny, the pistol, and the harvester), the steamboat had many different inventors, though posterity tends to emphasize only one: Robert Fulton. Following the debut of Fulton's steamboat *Clermont* in 1807, a growing fleet appeared on American rivers. Whereas a sail- or oar-driven boat might have taken weeks or months to travel from Cincinnati or St. Louis to Natchez, Mississippi, or New Orleans, a steamboat could make the same journey in a few days. Moreover, upriver travel had been all but impossible in older barges, but steamboats rapidly developed the capacity to move tons of freight upstream at a speed of about ten miles per hour. Steamboats proved such a useful mode of distribution that, by 1848, New Orleans had become the second-busiest port in the country, following New York City.

Cotton

Improvements in internal transportation greatly speeded the movement of agricultural goods to coastal cities for international export. Cotton was the fastest-growing export in the decades following independence. Cotton production was still quite small in the United States in the 1790s, but it became more significant than tobacco or sugar.

In 1793, Eli Whitney's patenting of a cotton gin helped trigger the rise of an "Empire of Cotton" in the southern United States. Whitney's invention made it possible to remove seeds from cotton fiber approximately fifty times faster than before, enabling the acceleration in US cotton production in the early nineteenth century. American cotton exports soared from accounting for a value of about $5 million, or 16 percent of the total of American exports, in 1800 to a value of about $200 million, or 60 percent, in 1860.

The sale of cotton brought wealth to a new class of plantation owners, financiers, and brokers. It also increased the reliance of the Southern economy on commercial agriculture and slavery and dampened its industrial development. Although some cotton producers did not depend on slave labor, large plantation owners often had more than 50 slaves and sometimes 100 or 200 spread over several plantations. Enslaved persons were legally defined, and bought and sold, as property. By 1860, a male "hand" would sell for $1,800. By that year the total value of the slave population was $3 billion, three times the amount invested in US manufacturing.

In 1807, Congress passed legislation banning the further importation of slaves into the United States. Though most support for this restriction came from abolitionists, some historians contend that slaveholders also favored this measure because it effectively increased the value of their slaves. Furthermore, the bill did not spell the end of the institution of slavery. Quite to the contrary, the slave population continued to grow. Moreover, the center of the slave population moved farther south. As plantation owners expanded cotton production into new territories, they purchased huge numbers of enslaved people from the upper South, forcing them to relocate, and, in the process, breaking up families and communities. Indeed, several new states that became part of the United States after 1800—including Louisiana (1812), Mississippi (1817), Alabama (1819), Missouri (1821), Arkansas (1836), Texas (1845), and Florida (1845)—became cotton-producing slave states.

As the American cotton industry grew, native peoples suffered further loss of their lands through violent theft by whites. The Creeks and Cherokees were displaced from their land in Alabama and Georgia to make way for cotton farms. The Chickasaw and Choctaw nations were removed from land in western Tennessee and as far south as Mississippi. These relocations were part of what is today known as the Trail of Tears, the large-scale dislocation of Native Americans from their homelands during the 1830s, most often to lands west of the Mississippi. During the Cherokee removal of 1838, more than 2,000 of the 16,000

Cherokees who were forced to relocate died on the arduous journey.

The productivity of cotton fields increased significantly over the period for many reasons, including the move to more fertile land and the improvement of seeds, which made cotton bolls easier to pick. The rise in cotton production also corresponded with the increasingly brutal treatment of slaves, as overseers attempted to maximize the output of each slave. Cruelty was methodical and deeply ingrained in the plantation system. Plantation owners and overseers collected and analyzed data from their hands and compared production across years. Some cotton planters in the antebellum years relied on careful bookkeeping practices to manage their plantations. Thomas Affleck's *Cotton Plantation Record and Account Book* (published around 1850) taught standardized record-keeping methods and calculations—such as pounds of cotton produced per acre and the gross and net value of production—and even urged the keeping of statistics on the lives and deaths of slaves, their use of clothing and tools, and their productivity over time.

The growing demand for cotton triggered the rise of an extensive network of intermediaries and brokers. Planters shipped their raw cotton to a cotton factor, who not only purchased the planter's crops but also provided credit and supplies. The factor then sold the cotton to manufacturers or shipped it to other middlemen along the route to Liverpool—the hub of the nineteenth-century textile industry—or to New England. Many of these cotton brokers, such as Henry Lehman (who immigrated to the United States from Bavaria in 1844 and went on to found the financial services firm Lehman Brothers), made their livelihoods in the booming cotton industry of the mid-nineteenth century.

The sale of cotton brought many links between the slave-labor system in the South and the free-labor system in the North. Northern factories made agricultural tools such as rakes and plows for plantations, and Northern insurance companies insured slave owners against the loss of their human "property." The products of slavery—tobacco and cotton, especially—went to supply Northern factories.

Despite deep connections to New York finance and New England textile mills, Southern cotton plantations lagged in adopting, in equal measure, the innovative technology that by the 1840s and 1850s was reshaping the North, including manufacturing machinery. Moreover, although plantations were profitable for the slave owners and their middlemen, they were costly for society. Slave patrols, for instance, monitored and policed much of the South to try to apprehend runaways. Slavery was also, needless to say, a moral blight. Indeed, many Europeans who visited the United States were struck by the stark contradictions inherent in American society, which tolerated the institution of slavery in a land supposedly founded on the virtue of equality. In 1842, while touring the United States, Charles Dickens, reflecting on the cruelty of slavery, lamented the state of the Republic: "Rather, for me, restore the forest and the Indian village."

Whale oil

Like the production and sale of raw cotton, the processing and marketing of whale oil became a global business in the first half of the nineteenth century. The industry, which supplied the fuel for the illumination of many cities and provided lubrication for manufacturing machinery in the production of textiles and other industries, also brought fortunes to American entrepreneurs, who dominated the industry. At the time of the American Revolution, there were about 360 whaling vessels (and roughly 9,000 men) engaged in whaling. By 1840, that number had nearly doubled to 700 vessels—accounting for over three-fourths of all whaling ships operating around the globe.

Even before the Revolutionary War, whale oil and baleen (used in the manufacture of umbrellas, whips, and corsets) were among the colonies' most significant exports to Britain. Around 1750, merchants in Rhode Island and Nantucket began separating the waxy spermaceti and oil of the "head matter." The resultant oil was of the highest quality, and spermaceti candles were marketed (and priced) as a luxury item because they burned with less smoke and odor than tallow candles and gave a brighter light. George Washington and Thomas Jefferson both specified spermaceti candles for their homes.

New England ports dominated the whaling industry—especially New Bedford, the island of Nantucket, and Provincetown, Massachusetts. Whalers sailed to the Cape Verde Islands, South America, Japan, and Alaska and the Bering Strait, as well as into the Arctic Ocean. Whaling was, moreover, a capital-intensive industry. In 1850, a New Bedford whaling venture required a capital investment between $20,000 and $30,000—far more than that needed for the average American farm at that time ($2,258) and more, too, than the average manufacturing firm ($4,335). But a good haul yielded a high return, as evidenced by the large mansions that sprung up around the port of New Bedford in the early nineteenth century.

Whaling "agents" started ventures and organized the necessary capital. They acquired a ship and worked with the captain to settle on the crew and equipment. They purchased insurance because whaling was riskier than many kinds of trade: ships could be lost at sea or catch on fire, or captains could experience mutiny. The agents picked out the type of whales to target and the route. Crew members with various skills—coopers, carpenters, cooks, stewards, skilled and semiskilled seamen—were contracted for a fraction of the voyage's profits. Payment took the form of a *lay*, or a percentage of the net returns from a trip. A harpooner, for instance, might receive one-ninetieth lay.

2. Whaleships and casks of whale oil at Central Wharf in New Bedford, Massachusetts, about 1870. Since colonial times, whale oil had been used for illumination in homes, lighthouses, streets, and shops.

The technology of whaling improved over the decades. In the late eighteenth century, whalers began building tryworks—furnaces for melting blubber—on the boats, so that a whale could be processed at sea rather than hauled back to port. The size of the main vessels doubled, with smaller whaleboats used to attack the whale. Harpooning also changed. Initially, the harpoons were attached to log floats, which were meant to stay afloat during the hunt, but often allowed the whale to swim away if oarsmen failed to keep up. In the 1760s, whalers began to attach the harpoon directly to the ship. This proved dangerous—sperm whales can swim at twenty-five miles per hour and dive deep into the ocean—but it did increase the rate of capture. Still, the dangers associated with whaling were well known, immortalized in Herman Melville's classic *Moby-Dick*, published in 1851.

By the 1830s, American fisheries were annually producing about 4.7 million gallons of fine sperm oil, 5.8 million gallons of regular whale oil, and 1.6 million pounds of whalebone. The industry peaked in 1845–46 and then steadily declined as a result of foreign competition, the discovery of petroleum-based lubricants, and, after the mid-1860s, the destruction of a significant portion of the whaling fleet during the Civil War. However, some companies survived. Nye Lubricants, Inc., founded in 1844, even went on to supply lubricants for NASA spaceships in the twentieth century.

The fur trade

Like the oceans, America's forests were also a source of profit for entrepreneurs. One especially lucrative industry was the trade in animal hides, furs, skins, and pelts. Since 1608, French trappers were active in the North American woods along the St. Lawrence River, and the Dutch and English trapped and traded furs (mostly beaver) along the Hudson River in New York. In both British settlements in the Northeast and French outposts in the upper Midwest, Europeans depended on Native Americans, who had long-established trading networks, extensive geographical knowledge, and skill in trapping animals and processing furs. The scale of production was staggering. By the early 1800s, estimates placed the number of furs and pelts exported per year at around 200,000.

John Jacob Astor became one of the most prominent figures in the trade. Astor was a German-born musical instrument maker who moved to England before sailing to New York around 1784. He met a fur trader on the voyage to North America and, even while working in his brother's butcher shop, was inspired to purchase and resell furs. Astor set up a shop selling musical instruments and simultaneously began making trips to western New York, seeking out European and Native American trappers to acquire furs to sell in his shop.

At this time, Montreal was a center of the fur-trading industry because of its location on the St. Lawrence River and access to the Great Lakes. To gain a larger share of furs and pelts compared to rival Canadian companies, Astor began trading in the Pacific Northwest. There, he worked with Russian traders to acquire seal and sea otter pelts. He also established an overland route to ship furs and pelts from the west, using a set of posts along the route traveled by Lewis and Clark in their expedition of 1804–6. Astor achieved a milestone in 1808 when he acquired a New York state–issued corporate charter to establish the American Fur Company. Astor always treated the concern, though technically a corporation, as something closer to a partnership, with few significant investors.

The War of 1812 disrupted Astor's commercial plans, but he still succeeded in building an international network. His fur-trading business (which also traded teas, sandalwood, opium, and other items) reached its height in the late 1810s to the early 1830s, with ships traveling to China, Spain, the Netherlands, Germany, Cuba, and Brazil. However, by 1833, Astor was seventy years old and his health was declining. He withdrew from the American Fur Company in 1834, and it was defunct by 1847.

Astor's legacy, however, endured. His dominance in the continental fur trade and his subsequent investments in banking, insurance, and especially New York real estate prefigured the next stage of the American economy—an era of geographic expansion and economic growth. Astor became the model of a business tycoon, who made use of the corporation as an organizational form, invested in property, was socially prominent, and acquired an extensive library later given to the public. (Astor's library was eventually merged with that of philanthropist James Lenox and others to form the New York Public Library.) The Astors became the first of several family dynasties whose origins were in business. They were soon followed by others, such as the Vanderbilts, Rockefellers, Morgans, and Mellons.

Chapter 3
Early manufacturers, 1820–1850

During the decades from 1820 to 1850, the American economy continued to grow, in terms of population (from around 10 to 23 million) and in the number of states (from twenty-three to thirty-one). In those same decades, the division between the North and South intensified. The plantation economy of the South continued to expand, and white planters came to form a Southern aristocracy with immense economic, political, and social power.

By contrast, manufacturing flourished in the mid-Atlantic and New England. The share of the labor force in manufacturing increased from 3.2 percent in 1810 to 14.5 percent in 1850. In terms of output, US manufacturers produced a range of goods including practical items—farm equipment, tools, guns, railroad tracks, and carriages—and cultural and decorative products for homes—pictures, books, carpets, clocks, and objects for the "parlor," a new feature of many homes.

In the early 1830s, Secretary of the Treasury Louis McLane conducted a survey on the state of American manufacturing in the North. McLane drew up a list of queries regarding the size of the operation, the types of raw materials and energy sources used, and the wages paid to employees. The survey included about 5,000 enterprises, with roughly 1,920 in Massachusetts, 1,180 in New Hampshire, and 500 in Pennsylvania. The most numerous types of manufacturers were textile mills (with 54,456 workers engaged in the industry), primary metal makers (24,297), and makers of leather products (23,817). In general, water remained the most common power source, but animal power was also frequently mentioned (in the form of horses, oxen, and mules). The survey also revealed the gradual increase in the use of coal, especially in Pennsylvania firms located near newly discovered coal mines.

Among the enterprises surveyed, most were organized as partnerships (rather than corporations), in part because capital requirements for firms remained small. Much manufacturing work was done by hand or with simple machines. Among the larger establishments were textile mills, metal producers, and leather works (often shoemakers), which employed an average of forty to fifty workers. Women and young men constituted a significant portion of the labor force in these manufacturing companies, totaling about 10 percent at the start of the century and running to roughly 40 percent by 1832. Most adult females— nearly 70 percent of those employed in manufacturing—worked in either the cotton or the wool textile industries. However, the proportion of women in the labor force overall decreased after 1850, as more adult males moved from agriculture to manufacturing.

E. I. du Pont de Nemours & Co., more commonly known as DuPont, was one of the largest companies of the period. A gunpowder manufactory, the company listed a total of 140 men working in its factories in 1831, including laborers, carters, and coopers. Laborers there worked twelve-hour days in the summer and nine-hour days in the winter. In the early 1830s, the company produced 850,000 pounds of gunpowder annually and calculated the value of land, buildings, water power, and machinery at $80,000 (or $2.1 million in 2020 dollars). It was dangerous work. DuPont reinvested a significant portion of its profits back into the company, in part to recover from explosions that occurred on company grounds during the testing of its powder.

Several firms made advances in agricultural machinery, the most important of which was the mechanical reaper. Cyrus McCormick—with the help of his father and an enslaved laborer named Jo Anderson, who worked on their Virginia plantation—invented a mechanical reaper to harvest crops in place of the handheld sickle. McCormick received a patent on his horse-driven device in the 1830s but did not produce a genuinely workable model until the early 1840s. The machine was especially well received by farmers working the flat land of the Midwest, and so, in 1847, McCormick moved his operation from Virginia to Chicago. Cyrus and his brother William supervised a factory there and built a network of salesmen who traveled the region demonstrating the machine to farmers and repairing reapers in the field.

The critical organizational development in the first decades of the nineteenth century was the expansion of the factory system. The factory brought workers to a single location to work together, created a specialized division of tasks and labor, and regulated the start and end of the workday.

Textiles

Entrepreneurs in the textile industry founded some of the earliest factories. The amount of capital necessary to establish a mill was relatively small—estimated by one entrepreneur to be about $10,000 in 1814 (or roughly $140,000 in 2020 dollars). Spinning mills were erected wherever there was enough water power to turn them, and the domestic textile industry proliferated. The country had "cotton mill fever," according to one observer. By 1810, there were some eighty-seven cotton textile mills in operation or under construction from Massachusetts to Virginia, most within thirty miles of Providence, Rhode Island.

In 1810, curious about the possibilities for producing cotton cloth in the United States, Massachusetts-born Francis Cabot Lowell traveled through England and Scotland to study the British textile industry. He and his family stayed for almost two years, during which time he visited many mills and committed to memory the design of the power looms, which ran by steam or water power. After his return to Massachusetts, he enlisted the skillful mechanic Paul Moody to recreate these machines, which became crucial for the industrial development of the United States.

Lowell invested in a small mill in Waltham, Massachusetts, and began producing cloth in late 1814. Together with Nathan Appleton, Patrick Tracy Jackson, and others, he founded the Boston Manufacturing Company, harnessing the power of the Charles River to run the machines. The mill was a significant innovation. Unlike most earlier mills, it was fully integrated, taking in raw cotton and performing all tasks of spinning and weaving to produce the final cloth. In 1815, Lowell and Moody secured a patent for the mechanized power loom they developed—one that featured improvements on the British designs. To finance their operations, Lowell and his associates sold shares of stock to their wealthy friends, creating a group of investors known as the Boston Associates.

In 1816, Lowell traveled to Washington, DC, to successfully lobby the federal government for tariffs on imported cloth. The Tariff of 1816 delivered to infant American industries the desired protection from overseas competition. However, the question of tariffs soon became a major source of conflict between the North and South, with the manufacturing North generally supporting tariffs as a way to grow industry and the export-driven South opposing them because they raised prices on imported finished goods. The debate over tariffs was one major issue in the lead-up to the Civil War.

The factories established by the Boston Associates pioneered not only technology but also a new program for managing labor. Recognizing that high wages paid to American men would substantially reduce the mills' profitability, Lowell and Appleton decided that they would recruit young women. They set up dormitories run by matrons, who charged workers a fixed rate for room and board and provided reassurance to the young women's families that they had adequate moral supervision. Most of the dormitories had a curfew of ten o'clock in the evening, and the girls were expected to attend church on Sundays.

Lowell, influenced by what he had observed of a conscientious program of "improvement" in Scotland, intended to create not only an efficient means of production but also a more salutary work culture than existed in the "dark Satanic mills" of the British industry, as poet William Blake had called them. Lowell's partner, Nathan Appleton, described the way that the Boston Associates envisioned the place of their business in the political economy: "By adding to the means of comfort and happiness in the laboring classes, their character and standing in society is elevated, and they are better fitted to discharge the duties of good citizens." This early manifestation of corporate philanthropy differed significantly from methods pursued by later business leaders.

To some observers, this relatively benign arrangement eliminated some of the worst abuses that troubled the British textile industry. Charles Dickens, visiting Lowell in 1842, wrote that the mill workers "were healthy in appearance, many of them remarkably so, and had the manners and deportment of young women: not of degraded brutes of burden."

Although these workers might have been less desperate than their British counterparts, the conditions were hard. Girls worked from five o'clock in the morning to seven o'clock in the evening six days a week in noisy, hot factories. Such conditions ultimately led to restiveness. After wage cuts during the economic depressions of the 1830s, women millworkers organized several strikes and eventually formed the Lowell Female Labor Reform Association in 1845. Strikes, however, proved largely unsuccessful. Participants were fired and often blacklisted by employers. In the 1840s, the textile mills began to transition to immigrant male labor—a shift made possible by an influx of immigrants to the United States, in particular from Ireland following the potato famine of 1845–49.

Other industries, such as shoes and boots, also began to flourish in New England around this time thanks to the ability to mechanize parts of the production process. Lynn, Massachusetts, had been a center for shoe manufacturing since the colonial period. By the end of the eighteenth century, Lynn shoemakers were making 170,000 pairs per year, and the industry had spread to neighboring towns. This growth was made possible by several innovations in the 1840s allowing the cutting, eyehole-punching, and sole-shaping processes to be mechanized.

In addition to Massachusetts, New York City also became a hub of the textile industry. The city's garment district traces its roots back to the early nineteenth century, when city tailors began to produce large amounts of clothing for the growing population of enslaved plantation workers in the South. This marked the beginning of the transition from handmade to ready-made clothing in the United States, spurred by the introduction of the sewing machine in the 1850s. By the 1860s, most Americans purchased, rather than made, their clothes.

Firearms

Factory production also transformed the firearms industry, initially in the government-owned federal armory. In 1777, George Washington chose Springfield, Massachusetts, as the site for an armory to provide firearms to his troops during the American Revolution because the city was strategically located along the

Connecticut River and also on roads to Boston, New York City, and Albany. The arsenal manufactured cannons, muskets, and other weapons.

The Springfield Armory became famous during Shays' Rebellion, an (ultimately unsuccessful) uprising led by farmer Daniel Shays in 1786–87. With 4,000 followers, he attempted to storm the armory and overthrow the Massachusetts state government in protest of inflation and taxation. Not long afterward, however, the armory became famous for another reason: the manufacture of high-quality firearms through the use of interchangeable parts.

The idea of interchangeable parts caught the attention of leading inventors and entrepreneurs as early as the 1770s and 1780s. Thomas Jefferson became a promoter of the concept while in France as he observed standardized manufacturing by the French military. He described it in a letter to John Jay in 1785:

> An improvement is made here in the construction of the musket....It consists in the making every part of them so exactly alike that what belongs to any one, may be used for every other musket in the magazine....A workman...presented me the parts of 50 locks taken to pieces, and arranged them in compartments. I put several together myself taking pieces at hazard as they came to hand, and they fitted in the most perfect manner.

In 1815, Colonel Roswell Lee, the newly appointed superintendent of the Springfield Armory, worked toward the realization of interchangeable parts for musket manufacture in the United States. He introduced a system to carefully measure hand-manufactured parts, rather than assessing them by eye, both during and after the production process, to achieve complete uniformity. However, the goal of achieving true interchangeability remained elusive until the invention, in 1822, of stockmaking machinery, developed by Thomas Blanchard, an employee at the Springfield Armory. The machine, called the Blanchard lathe, was able to produce identical gunstocks. To fully mechanize the production process, Blanchard developed other devices (fourteen in all) to carve the recess for the barrel and make the lock and mortise for the trigger mechanism. These inventions made hand labor on these parts virtually obsolete. Similar innovations were soon introduced at the second armory commissioned by the US government, the Harpers Ferry Armory, established about five years after the one at Springfield.

Both armories developed elements of large-scale manufacturing: the reliance on machines to produce standardized parts, a division of labor, and a system of quality control inspections. Both also relied on decades of government contracts to fund the research and development of this new technology. Having a guaranteed, up-front source of funding was critical, because at this time interchangeability was extremely costly. The US government, and specifically the War Department, was willing to make such a large investment because of how poorly the US arsenal had fared in the War of 1812, when the army destroyed many weapons with small defects that might have been salvaged by the ability to insert interchangeable parts.

Beginning in the 1840s, arms manufacturing switched from mainly public auspices to private ones. Several private arms manufacturers adopted the systems developed at government armories and refined them to form profitable factories. In 1836, Samuel Colt patented technology for mass-producing six-shooter revolvers. Colt had worked on a whaling ship and claimed that the winding of rope aboard the ship gave him the idea for the barrel revolver for which his company would later be renowned. The key innovation was in the breech of the gun. Where other pistols had a single chamber breech, Colt's breech rotated automatically such that it could fire six bullets in rapid succession.

Colt's innovations were important not only in America's industrial revolution but also in marketing and promotion. He stamped each revolver with his name and toured Europe and other parts of the globe promoting his guns and delivering ornate firearms to leading political and royal figures. He advertised heavily in newspapers about the "Romance of a Colt," gave interviews, and told stories to the press, calling the new revolver "the world's right arm." The Colt revolver became a crucial part of the legend of the American West.

Clocks

In addition to textiles and firearms, the clock industry also adopted systems of factory production. In the eighteenth century, clocks were luxury goods—a tall clock was generally the most expensive item in the home of a wealthy colonist. Clockmakers could produce perhaps twenty-five clocks a year, which sold at the high price of about $25 (about $825 in 2020 dollars) without the wooden case. Clockmaking, like whaling, was an early entrepreneurial industry clustered in a few locations—in the case of clocks, in central Connecticut. In the early nineteenth century, Eli Terry, a Connecticut clockmaker, developed a method of producing clocks in greater volume and at a lower cost.

Terry pursued technical innovation, including efforts to make clocks with wooden works rather than brass and the development of a simplified production process that would make it possible for unskilled workers, rather than trained artisans, to assemble the timepieces. For more complicated tasks, he began using apprentices to roughly cut wooden parts that could then be refined by skilled craftsmen. In addition, Terry paid attention to design features. He used inexpensive paper dials glued to wood and then employed women skilled at painting to create the clock faces. He also deployed water power to replace handsaws.

Along with innovations in production and decoration, Terry implemented a new system of distribution that allowed him to build demand for his clocks. He employed a network of independent peddlers to sell his wares. These peddlers headed out with samples of clocks and visited farmhouses throughout the country, including the rural South. They would take orders and then return to deliver the clock and collect payment.

Some peddlers used clever tactics, such as asking skeptical farmers to keep an unsold clock on their walls as a favor for a month or two while the peddler traveled about, hoping that the farmer would become dependent on the invention and decide to buy one. These and other sales tactics made clock peddlers the subject of humorous tales. Indeed, one of the first "businessmen" to appear in North American literature was *Sam Slick, the Clockmaker* (1836). Canadian author Thomas Haliburton endowed Sam Slick with colorful use of language, which he used to manipulate potential customers into a purchase—a skill shared with other fictional salesmen of later periods, such as Sinclair Lewis's *Babbitt* (1922). The peddlers were so successful in their approaches, wrote Haliburton, that "the house of every substantial farmer had three substantial ornaments, a wooden clock, a tin reflector [oven], and a Polyglot Bible" sold by a peddler. By 1820, American clockmakers were producing and selling about 15,000 clocks annually.

The American System

The products of American manufacturers were prominently on display at the 1851 Crystal Palace Exhibition in London, which featured waterwheels, steam engines, and other sources of power, as well as inventions such as Colt's repeating arms. After the exhibition, two Englishmen—Joseph Whitworth, an accomplished engineer, and George Wallis, an expert in industrial design—were appointed by the British government to visit America. They toured centers of American manufacturing in the summer of 1853. Around the time of Wallis and Whitworth's tour, the leading manufacturing industries in the United States were boots and shoes, cotton goods, men's clothing, lumber, iron, machinery, woolen goods, carriages, flour and meal, and leather goods.

As they observed, the "American System of Manufactures" emphasized standardized parts, highly mechanized production methods, and a preference for practicality rather than luxury. Whitworth and Wallis described these characteristics in their report: "The American manufacturer…is in some respects wiser than his foreign competitor, and in many instances leaves the ultra-ornate to be supplied from Birmingham and Sheffield, and directs his energies to the development of a better and less exuberant style, which he finds is demanded by the more refined amongst his countrymen."

The reputation of American manufacturers grew overseas as they began to use the same skills, processes, and strategies they developed at home to sell goods abroad. Some even began to open branches in other countries. From 1800 to 1860, about 600 American entrepreneurs went abroad, to countries including Canada, England, Mexico, Cuba, Argentina, Paraguay, Hawaii, and Russia. Most foreign operations took the form of sales offices or factories, in fields ranging from brick manufacturing to heavy machinery—including paper mills, carriage works, and lumber. These entrepreneurs set an important precedent in the transformation from merchants to multinationals through the early planting of stakes abroad.

Chapter 4
Railroads and mass distribution, 1850–1880

The decades after 1850, and especially following the Civil War (1861–65), ushered in a period of unprecedented economic innovation, productivity, and societal transformation in the United States with the advent of new sources of energy, new methods of communication, and new modes of transportation. This period of growth continued well into the twentieth century, completely revolutionizing the business landscape in the United States.

In energy, one significant change was the growing use of coal as a source of power. Anthracite coal, a harder, cleaner-burning variety than the more common bituminous coal, was prized for use in factories and homes. Bituminous coal was used in the production of coke, a porous fuel used in steel blast furnaces. By mid-century, Pittsburgh emerged as the central market for both types of coal.

In communication, the invention of the telegraph in the 1840s made the delivery of messages and news, even across continents, nearly instantaneous. In 1844, Samuel Morse sent the now-famous first telegraph message, "What hath God wrought," from the Capitol Building in Washington, DC, to Baltimore. By 1851, there were more than fifty telegraph companies operating in the United States. Just ten years later, in 1860, more than 2,000 miles

of telegraph lines connected cities across much of the
United States.

Innovations in both energy and communication found application
in the most important industry of the period—the railroad.
Increases in coal production accelerated the construction of
railway lines, while telegraphs improved the ease and efficiency of
communication, making it possible to manage large businesses
over vast spaces.

Railroads

In the late eighteenth and early nineteenth centuries, many
entrepreneurs and inventors experimented with new methods of
transportation. The most transformative was the steam-powered
locomotive. While the first locomotives were of British design,
American engineers quickly adapted the technology to the
American terrain and geography.

In the United States, the first railways were built in the 1820s.
State charters authorized entrepreneurs to undertake rail
transportation projects, including the 1826 Granite Railway, a
three-mile wooden railway using horses to haul granite to a
nearby river to supply the construction of the Bunker Hill
Monument in Charlestown, Massachusetts. Entrepreneurs in New
York, Maryland, and South Carolina soon constructed similar
short railways.

Railroads became an essential way for many American cities to
gain easier access to agricultural output and manufactured goods.
One of the first cities to capitalize on this technology was
Baltimore. Maryland-born businessmen Philip E. Thomas and
George Brown wanted to bring a railway to Baltimore to help the
city compete with New York after the building of the Erie Canal.
In 1830, they founded the Baltimore and Ohio Railroad, taking
passengers in cars pulled along by horses. Steam locomotives soon

replaced horses. Peter Cooper—builder of the first American steam locomotive, named the "Tom Thumb"—challenged a horse-drawn car to a race. The horse won, but Cooper nevertheless convinced the owners of the railroad of the potential of his new technology. The railroad line eventually became one of the nation's largest, reaching the Ohio River in 1852 and ultimately opening stations in twelve states and the District of Columbia.

Initially, there were numerous small railroads built to connect major cities to outlying towns—Boston to Lowell, Newburyport, and Providence; Camden to Amboy; Philadelphia to Reading and Baltimore. In the 1840s, more reliable construction methods began to make railroad technologies better and more uniform, allowing railways to supplant canals and turnpikes for transporting passengers and freight.

Rail transport had many advantages over canals and steamboats. Trains could move goods in all seasons and all weather, and, above all, they traveled comparatively fast. The trip from New York to Chicago, which would have taken at least three weeks in 1840, took only three days by 1857; a trip from Boston to New York or New York to Washington took only a day.

Cornelius Vanderbilt pioneered in railroad building and consolidation. Vanderbilt was born into a poor family on Staten Island, New York, just a few years after the ratification of the Constitution, and lived through the Civil War and Reconstruction eras. At age eleven, he was helping with his father's ferry business. By age twenty, he had bought his own boat and was competing to establish routes along the East Coast. He was a tenacious competitor and frequently undercut established shipping companies by offering lower prices until they folded—and then he would often raise rates. He was bold enough to challenge a steamboat monopoly that had been granted by New York State to Robert Livingston and Robert Fulton, two early and prominent figures in the industry. Vanderbilt was able to break their monopoly and then expanded his ferry services, including the operation of a steamboat from New Jersey to New York. Succeeding in his ferry services, including ownership of the Staten Island Ferry, Vanderbilt also entered the business of oceangoing steamboat services following the discovery of gold in California. Then, he turned his attention to the most exciting technology of his generation: the railroad.

During the 1850s, Vanderbilt bought stock in several railways, including the Erie Railway, the Central Railroad, the Hartford and New Haven, and the New York and Harlem. By 1864, Vanderbilt gained control of the Hudson River Railroad and, in 1867, the New York Central Railroad. In 1869, he began construction of Grand Central Depot as the terminal of his New York Central Railroad, which connected New York City with Boston, Chicago, and St. Louis. (It became Grand Central Terminal in 1913 and now is adorned by an 8 1/2-foot statue of the "Commodore," as he was known.) When he died, Vanderbilt was said to control more than a tenth of the entire capital of the United States.

Another pioneer was the industrialist and civil engineer John Edgar Thomson of the Pennsylvania Railroad. In terms of sheer size, the Pennsylvania Railroad, established in 1846, became the most extensive railroad in the world. Thomson was chief engineer and president of the Pennsylvania Railroad and built rails across the Allegheny Mountains to connect Harrisburg and Pittsburgh. Thomson also oversaw the financial and organizational challenges of growing the railroad west to Ohio and east to Philadelphia. To do this, Thomson introduced new technology, turning from wood to coal for fuel and from iron to steel for rails and cars. Like Vanderbilt, Thomson acquired many other railroads, canals, and shipping companies. Before the end of the century, one could travel to a wide range of US cities on the Pennsylvania Railroad, including Chicago, New York, Philadelphia, Pittsburgh, Toledo, St. Louis, and Washington.

The government facilitated the growth of the railroads. From 1855 to 1871, a US government land grant system allotted 129 million acres to railroad companies. This allowed the opening of railways from Chicago and Omaha all the way to San Francisco. Starting around the middle of the nineteenth century, many Americans and immigrants pushed west on railways as the discovery of mineral ores (or even just the rumors of such discoveries) attracted miners and opportunists. So-called boomtowns sprang up around mines all over the West—capitalizing on the need for supplies, wagons, and mining equipment—and saw significant increases in population in just a few years. After James Marshall discovered gold at Sutter's Mill in 1848, "forty-niners" rushed to California from all parts of the United States and abroad. San Francisco, which had only 1,000 residents in 1848, grew to 36,000 by 1852. Chinese immigrants, in particular, flocked to California goldfields in the thousands.

By the end of the 1860s, railroads traversed the nation. On May 10, 1869, Central Pacific Railroad Company president Leland Stanford drove the ceremonial golden spike that linked the Union Pacific and Central Pacific to form the first transcontinental railroad. Stanford embodied the combination of money, government, and industry that had together achieved this feat. Along with his brothers, Stanford had gone to California during the Gold Rush, making money as a partner in mining companies and as a storekeeper selling tools and supplies for miners. He became involved in California politics, helping to establish the Republican Party and, in 1861, was elected governor of the state. Stanford's platform for the gubernatorial nomination included an endorsement of the effort to build the transcontinental railroad, and he was named the president of the Central Pacific railroad during his candidacy. His legislative record was decidedly friendly to railroads, and despite some opposition, he pressed for subsidies and substantial loans to the Central Pacific in its bid to expand and connect with an eastern line. Like Vanderbilt, Stanford invested in steamships, and the Central Pacific Company controlled river traffic on the Colorado and profited from oceangoing trade into and out of San Francisco.

Railroad management

Given their unprecedented scope and scale, railroads brought changes to the structure and organization of business. One was the promotion of a growing profession—the salaried manager. Once railroads spanned distances of a hundred miles or more, managing them required new modes of communication. Schedules, budgets, and procedures could no longer be worked out by colleagues in a single office. Failure to coordinate the movement of trains along a single track led to costly and sometimes fatal collisions. Railroad owners began to respond to these conditions with new organizational structures, and the railroads also became one of the largest and earliest users of the telegraph to coordinate complex schedules. Indeed, as time went on, telegraph lines were increasingly laid or relocated along railroad tracks to assist with maintenance—a case of transportation and communication flourishing together.

Unlike the manufacturing firms of the early nineteenth century, the railroads employed thousands of people. With the growth of railroads came the need for managers to hire and train new personnel (most coming, at least in the early decades, from an agricultural background), to draft new rules for operation, to negotiate issues of finance and distribution, and to satisfy regulatory policies. Railroad companies were organized hierarchically, with managers working in separate departments to handle different administrative functions: president, treasurer, general superintendent, division superintendent, secretary, land agent, auditor, foreman, car inspector, master of engine repairs, and so on.

In 1855, Daniel McCallum, general superintendent of the New York and Erie Railroad, created a detailed organizational chart to show lines of authority within a single company, in a design reminiscent of the branches of a tree. A year later, in his report to the board, he articulated six principles of general administration, including "a proper division of responsibilities" and "the adoption of a system, as a whole, which will not only enable the general superintendent to detect errors immediately, but will also point out the delinquent." McCallum's report introduced ideas about channels of authority and communication that were critical to the growth of railroads and, later, of other large American businesses. Many of the large railroads subsequently adopted structures and procedures similar to those McCallum had pioneered at the New York and Erie.

In overseeing the operations of the railroad, managers encountered periods of labor unrest. When economic conditions worsened in the 1870s, especially with the Panic of 1873, some lines fell into bankruptcy and failed to pay their workers. The Great Railroad Strike of 1877, which lasted for more than a month, occurred after the Baltimore and Ohio reduced wages for the third time that year. Unrest spread to workers on other lines throughout the country.

The strike was part of a new phase in the development of organized labor in the United States at that time. The Knights of Labor, founded in 1869, espoused a broad platform advocating for the rights of all workers, including farmers. Membership grew rapidly in the 1870s, and the organization reached a peak membership of 700,000 in the mid-1880s. Around this time, however, a new labor organization founded by Samuel Gompers emerged, the American Federation of Labor, which was an alliance of craft unions. Gompers and the American Federation of Labor prioritized economic concerns, specifically working toward the "bread-and-butter" issues of wages, benefits, hours, and working conditions and advocating for the use of strikes and boycotts as a bargaining tool. The American Federation of

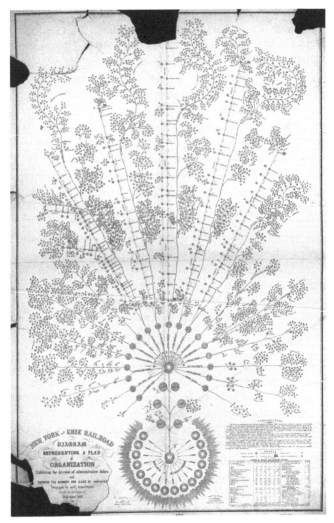

3. Daniel McCallum and George Holt Henshaw, "New York and Erie Railroad diagram representing a plan of organization," 1855. A tree-like organizational chart of the railroad shows the towns and stations covered in the plan's spreading branches, and the managerial and executive positions are shown in the circular roots below.

Labor came to embody the model for unionism in the United States.

Corporations

Along with management, railroads brought sweeping changes to the financial industry and spurred the creation of global capital markets. The largest railroads had initial capitalizations from $17 million to $35 million, compared to textile mills and metalworking factories that were rarely capitalized at over $1 million. Because railroads were so expensive to build, they could not be financed with local capital alone and thus provided ideal investment opportunities for Europeans with surplus capital looking to invest in the growing industries of North America.

To raise money more effectively, railroad leaders formed corporations, an organizational form that became increasingly common in the United States in the nineteenth century. Initial investors living in the region of a railroad frequently bought stock in the company, while European investors typically preferred bonds. Unexpected costs incurred by railroad companies often meant that the first sale of mortgage bonds was usually followed by a second and a third. In this way, railroads became a boon to financial markets. The railroads, too, created an opportunity for analysts like Henry Varnum Poor, who developed *Poor's Manual of Railroad Securities*, one of the first industrial journals, to inform those wishing to invest.

Railroad bonds and, to a lesser extent, stocks dominated Wall Street trading from the end of the Civil War to the beginning of the twentieth century. Those with money to risk often reaped great rewards—speculators, among them Daniel Drew, Jay Gould, and Jay Cooke, all made fortunes from their investments in railroads and even gained control of some railway lines. Trade and speculation surrounding these stocks and bonds contributed to the growth of the New York Stock Exchange (which was founded in 1817, but had not yet become dominant among other exchanges that existed at the time, including in Boston, Philadelphia, New Orleans, and Cincinnati).

However, railroad speculation could also have negative consequences for the national economy. Railroad speculation, corruption, and the sale of "watered stock," or shares issued at a greater value than justified by a company's assets, contributed to the Panic of 1873, a financial crisis in the United States and Europe that lasted several years.

Mass distribution

Railroads had a significant impact not just on management and finance but also on distribution. Commerce that had previously relied on rivers running from north to south now traveled on rail from east to west. The railroads enabled large-scale settlement in the Midwest, and they helped to create the beginnings of a national market, which made a difference in many areas of commerce, including in the quality and availability of food. Whereas Americans living in rural areas previously had to depend on homegrown food, grocers could now expect regular shipments of flour, spices, and many other foods from distant wholesalers.

Chain stores were one new form of organization to emerge during this period. Making use of the railroad, the Great Atlantic & Pacific Tea Company, an early chain store, began operation in 1859. The first location—a small store in New York City—expanded to sixteen cities by the time its founder retired in 1878. By 1900, the chain had grown to 200 stores in twenty-eight states. In 1879, F. W. Woolworth opened the first of its five-and-ten-cent discount stores in Lancaster, Pennsylvania. By 1904, there were 120 stores operating in twenty-one states.

Mail-order stores, too, got their start at this time, enabled by advances in the postal system and the expansion of the rail network, which increased the speed of delivery while reducing the cost of postage. For example, in 1847, railroads carried just 10 percent of mail and postage cost five cents an ounce within a range of 300 miles. By 1857, railroads carried roughly a third of all mail, and postage rates had dropped to three cents an ounce for a range of 3,000 miles.

Aaron Montgomery Ward built the first large catalog sales business beginning in 1872, when he introduced a single-page catalog. By 1887, the catalog had grown to more than 500 pages and advertised some 24,000 products. By the turn of the century, the catalog was nearly 1,000 pages in length, and annual sales reached $7 million. Competition soon came from Richard Sears, who began selling watches by mail in 1886, with partner Alvah Roebuck. In the recession of 1893, Aaron Nusbaum and Julius Rosenwald became partners of Sears, Roebuck and Company, and Rosenwald played a major role in expanding the line of goods and managing the mail-order operations. It took Sears only a few years to overtake Montgomery Ward in terms of profits—through analytical management, savvy advertising, and low prices. By 1900, there were more than 1,200 mail-order companies in the United States.

The advent of Parcel Post for package delivery in 1913 again revolutionized the marketplace, especially in rural areas, where it vastly extended coverage. The Post Office handled more than 4 million packages on the first day of this service. It was a boon to farmers, especially—providing access to a much wider variety of goods at competitive prices—and allowed established businesses like Sears to expand their offerings dramatically.

A third type of innovative channel of distribution appeared in these decades: the department store. In 1858, Rowland Hussey Macy opened R. H. Macy & Co. in New York City on Sixth Avenue between 13th and 14th Streets. In 1902, the store moved to its current location in Herald Square. Philadelphia's Wanamaker's department store similarly had its start in the mid-nineteenth century. In 1875, John Wanamaker purchased a former Pennsylvania Railroad station to use as a massive retail location. These ornate department stores offered new and innovative sales policies. Macy's, for instance, created a one-price policy to put an end to haggling. Wanamaker's provided a money-back guarantee.

Department stores also sprang up farther west. In the 1850s, twenty-one-year-old Marshall Field moved from Massachusetts to Chicago and began working in a dry goods store. He later traversed the countryside as a traveling salesman, one of a swarm of so-called drummers who took sample cases from large wholesale houses to visit county stores throughout the United States. With the increasing number of such salesmen, rural merchants no longer had to make annual trips to large cities to purchase their inventory. In 1865, Field entered into a partnership with Potter Palmer and Levi Leiter to establish a new emporium, known as Field, Palmer, Leiter & Company. In 1879, the retail business moved to a new six-story building in downtown Chicago designed in French Second Empire style, with a mansard roof and sizeable central skylight. By 1881, Potter had withdrawn from the business and Field bought out Leiter's shares, renaming the company Marshall Field & Company. Around this time, the store had 34 departments, including dress goods, notions, and gloves. It would have more than 100 departments by the turn of the century. In the 1880s, the store introduced a bargain basement, which proved so popular that it accounted for nearly one-third of sales. Field and one of his top executives, Harry Gordon Selfridge, tried to make shoppers feel welcome in the store by having clerks be courteous and greet frequent customers by name. (Selfridge later developed these and other qualities in his London-based department store.)

In addition to commercial products, the railroads also enabled the secure transport of heavy agricultural machinery and machine tools. The McCormick Harvesting Machine Company benefitted

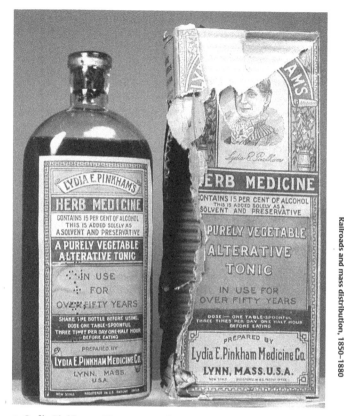

4. Lydia Pinkham, of Lynn, Massachusetts, created popular herbal tonics and vegetable compounds, often containing alcohol, for women. Along with other patent medicine makers, Pinkham was a brilliant promoter of her products, which featured ornate labels.

greatly from the railroad, especially after 1890, when many local lines had been developed in the Midwest and West. "It is perhaps needless to say that as soon as a railway penetrated a new district, one of the first passengers to alight at a hitherto isolated community was a McCormick representative looking for a dealer," the company reported proudly. By linking entrepreneurial farmers with innovative manufacturers, the railroad transformed the prairies into farmland.

The railroads, finally, also carried businesspeople and speculators working on a smaller scale, including patent medicine canvassers. Patent medicines, though seldom actually patented, were potions marketed to cure a variety of ailments. Many were some mixture of vegetable compounds and alcohol. Lydia E. Pinkham's Vegetable Compound, once a home herbal remedy, became wildly popular in the 1870s. In advertisements, the compound was said to be "a positive cure for all the painful complaints and weaknesses so common to our best female population." Patent medicines were also marketed through traveling medicine shows, which solicited testimonials and displayed colorful posters with exaggerated claims about products. These shows, including others like the popular Kickapoo Indian Medicine show, were forerunners of the modern advertising industry.

When the thirteen original states became one republic, they adopted the motto "*E Pluribus Unum*": from many, one. The railroads and telegraph made this motto real in a new, unforeseeable way—allowing the nation to become increasingly integrated into a single large marketplace even, ironically, as the country itself continued to expand geographically. These advances in technology were especially important for the growth of American business, as both railroads and telegraph enabled the founding, and management, of the large industrial concerns that came to dominate the economy over the next half century and more.

Chapter 5
An industrial country, 1880–1910

In the late nineteenth century, America's cities, linked by telegraph and railroad, grew at prodigious rates. The fastest growing was Chicago, which went from a fairly small town in 1840 (whose population was less than 5,000) to the second largest city in the United States (with nearly 1.1 million people) by 1890. The population increased to over 2 million by 1910. Other midwestern cities, like Minneapolis, Cleveland, Milwaukee, and Detroit, also grew by a factor of ten or more during this period, and some far greater than that. These cities became home to thousands of new businesses, including restaurants, laundries, hardware stores, and much else, and to large pools of laborers, many of whom were immigrants. In 1865, a Chicago business directory listed, for example, 768 grocers, 354 shoe- and bootmakers, 156 carpenters, and 481 boarding houses, among many other enterprises. The South remained agricultural and mostly rural. In 1910, the North had three cities with more than 1 million people each, yet the largest city in the South, by a wide margin, was New Orleans, with about 340,000.

After the Civil War, with much of the South in ruins, former slaves, now freedmen, sought to enter business and trades or find other ways to support themselves and their families. Freedmen, especially those who had served in the Union army, had hoped for land grants as compensation for their labor and service. Union

General William Tecumseh Sherman's field order issued in the waning months of the war seemed to indicate that they would receive "forty acres and a mule." Land redistribution on this scale had the potential to help make the free black population (which numbered around 3.9 million) economically self-sufficient, not only granting them land for their own use but also endowing them with a source of wealth that could be passed down to future generations. However, these promises failed to materialize. President Andrew Johnson—who assumed the office after Abraham Lincoln's assassination in 1865—was sympathetic to white Southern opposition and immediately revoked Sherman's order.

As a result, many freedmen found themselves stuck in a system of sharecropping and oppression that became widespread in the South. Landowners provided a plot on their plantation to work and supplies, and the sharecropping farmer received a share of the crop, perhaps one-half or one-third. Sharecropping, which endured through the 1950s, was a highly unequal system. African Americans who sought to create their businesses also faced tremendously adverse circumstances. Jim Crow laws meant they had to operate in segregated sections of cities, could not access credit markets, and had to sell to a smaller, often poor, clientele.

The Civil War had many consequences beyond the South. The war boosted Northern industry, and the aftermath saw the emergence of the New York Stock Exchange as a dominant financial institution. The postwar years also saw mining become a major industry in the West. Copper mining at Bingham County, Utah, and other locations was highly mechanized and the movement of coal, metals, and minerals from mines to factories became part of the geography of American industry. But perhaps the most significant change to the American business landscape from 1880 to 1910 was the rise of large industrial corporations, which produced in great volume and were led by a corps of managers. These new industrial concerns were enabled by technological advancements in machine production, a federal government that often sided with business over organized labor, and new laws, especially those that allowed for general incorporation.

Leading these large-scale operations were the so-called robber barons—known also, more positively though less frequently, as "captains of industry"—who forged colossal businesses in oil, steel, aluminum, meatpacking, and other industries. This generation of business leaders, including John D. Rockefeller, Andrew Carnegie, Henry Clay Frick, Andrew W. Mellon, J. P. Morgan, and James Buchanan Duke, followed in the path of Astor and Vanderbilt, marshaling financial, managerial, political, technological, and organizational skill to build their enterprises. They also relied on the work of previous generations of entrepreneurs who had built railroads, steamships, and telegraph lines that would allow them to create business empires.

All of these industrial companies started as small and entrepreneurial concerns, often with many competitors. As their businesses grew, these entrepreneurs, and the managers they hired, faced tremendous organizational challenges, most important, how to maintain continuous mass production for a national or international market. Yet, combining large-scale production and distribution was not one problem but several: securing a steady supply of raw materials, obtaining financing, and establishing reliable manufacturing processes. To solve production problems, manufacturers took advantage of new machines to transform the production process, producing goods at an unprecedented rate and realizing declining marginal costs (a phenomenon known as economies of scale). They also created highly standardized products, including commodities that were produced continuously (such as oil), branded goods (such as cigarettes), and complex machines (such as cash registers).

These manufacturers, too, faced challenges with distributing their products. Some responded by building vast networks of wholesale distribution, others by managing the process of reaching customers directly, and still others by relying entirely on middlemen and agents. The large industrial firms also experimented with different types of legal structures. Many began as partnerships, and some remained so for many decades. Others operated under a new legal structure called a *trust* or holding company, which allowed a small group of trustees to manage the activities of several companies. However, after the passage of a general incorporation law in New Jersey in 1896 and Delaware in 1899, most firms became limited liability corporations—the standard legal form for modern industrial enterprises.

The companies that rose to the top in their respective industries—notably Standard Oil, Carnegie Steel, Alcoa, Armour, Swift, and National Cash Register—were in some ways even more impressive than the railroads that facilitated their growth. They quickly became some of the largest business organizations the world had ever seen and gave rise to vast fortunes. John D. Rockefeller became the wealthiest person not only in the United States, as Astor and Vanderbilt had been in their time, but also in the world.

The industrialist managers who ran the large corporations of the late nineteenth century became so dominant in the American economy that the historian Alfred Chandler, looking back at this period from the 1970s, argued that the economy was no longer run by the invisible hand of the marketplace, as Adam Smith had observed, but by the "visible hand" of management.

Oil

Some of the first mass-production companies were producers of oil. Petroleum, or "rock oil" as it was first known, was initially used only in medicinal concoctions. But it began to serve as a substitute for whale oil in lubrication and illumination in the 1850s, especially after Edwin Drake's discovery of oil deposits in Titusville, Pennsylvania, in 1859. Indeed, annual production of crude oil, found in Pennsylvania, Ohio, West Virginia, and

Kentucky, rose from 1,000 barrels per day in 1860 to 14,000 barrels in 1870.

Unlike the early textile industry, which depended on water power for energy, the processing of oil required the high and steady heat of anthracite coal—mined in western Pennsylvania and made available through railway distribution. The heat from coal allowed for the continuous refining of oil, and the use of steam-driven engines hastened the flow of oil through pipelines in the production process. The processing of crude oil yielded kerosene, heavy fuels, and lubricants.

There were few regulations or legal requirements for entering the oil business, and the cost of entry was low. As a result, many entrepreneurs set out to build refineries in the decade after Titusville. The more ambitious sought to integrate their production capacity with the railroads by developing pipelines, large storage tanks, and special tank cars.

John D. Rockefeller was a wholesale grocer in Cleveland when he first entered the oil business as a side pursuit in 1863. By 1865, he had sold his grocery interest and partnered with English chemist Samuel Andrews—moving fully into the refining business with the new firm, Rockefeller and Andrews. The same year, they bought out the largest refinery in Cleveland and constructed a second refinery to increase output. Two years later, the firm added two new partners, Stephen Harkness and Henry Morrison Flagler, who contributed more than $100,000 to enable further growth. Harkness took no managerial role in the firm, but Flagler did, and he became one of Rockefeller's closest and most trusted business partners. By 1869, output had increased from 500 barrels a day to 1,500.

In 1870, Rockefeller combined facilities and reincorporated the firm as Standard Oil Company of Ohio, with a capitalization of $1 million. Rockefeller was the largest shareholder, owning slightly over one-quarter of the original 10,000 shares, and Andrews and Flagler each held roughly half that amount. The decision to become a corporation was strategic, making it easier to finance expansion without risking the loss of control over the company. As a result, the new Standard Oil immediately began a new phase of growth, and with a different strategy: rather than paying for acquisitions in cash, Standard offered to compensate acquired firms through the exchange of stock. This offer was attractive to some because it allowed acquired firms to share in, and benefit from, Standard's success. In this way, Standard acquired five large and seven small firms by the end of 1871. By 1872, Standard Oil dominated the Cleveland market and controlled one-quarter of the total daily capacity of the US oil industry. By the 1880s, Rockefeller was also developing a market for Standard Oil products abroad.

Rockefeller improved efficiency by finding ways to sell even the waste products from his refineries. As a result of these and other strategies, he cut the price of kerosene in half from 1865 to 1870, making it accessible to middle- and working-class families. Whereas whale oil was only affordable for the wealthy, the availability of inexpensive kerosene broadened the use of oil for home lighting. The high volume of production gave Standard powerful leverage in rate negotiations with railroads compared to its competitors. This approach was, in turn, advantageous for the railroads because they were able to run trains with only oil cars and plan a steady flow of traffic. Standard also built its own pipelines, which provided necessary storage capacity, as well as a steadier flow of crude oil into refineries.

By 1882, the firm controlled some 20,000 domestic wells and 4,000 miles of pipeline and had more than 100,000 employees. That same year, Rockefeller sought to organize his disparate entities, spread across many states, into a manageable organization, the Standard Oil Trust, overseen by nine trustees, who controlled the stock of the many semi-independent enterprises. This "trust," at first a secret organization, set a template for the organization of many other industrial enterprises. In 1885, Standard Oil moved its headquarters to 26 Broadway in New York City.

Steel

While oil brought light and heat to cities, steel was used to build infrastructure. Indeed, the steel industry was essential for the construction of rails for the railroad, bridges, buildings (including new skyscrapers), factories, railcars, ships, and industrial machinery. The steel industry grew out of iron making, which dated back to colonial times. However, it was not until Sir Henry Bessemer, an English inventor and engineer, created a new steel-making process in the mid-1860s and 1870s that the steel industry took off. By 1876, eleven mills had adopted Bessemer converters, producing roughly a half million tons of steel per year. By the end of World War I, US production rose to 60 million tons per year, making the country the world's leading steel producer.

Andrew Carnegie, born in Dunfermline, Scotland, was an early adopter of the Bessemer technology. In 1848, at just thirteen, Carnegie immigrated with his parents to the United States and went to work as a bobbin boy in the cotton mill where his father worked. After a brief period as a telegraph messenger, he left to work for Thomas A. Scott, who was then a station agent of the Pennsylvania Railroad (but would go on to lead the railroad). Guided by Scott, Carnegie began investing part of his salary in bridge-building firms.

After the Civil War, Carnegie left the railroads. Through his connections with Scott and Edgar Thomson, he entered the ironworks industry and later moved into steel production. One major factor that prompted Carnegie to make this career transition was the passage of new legislation in 1870 that imposed a tariff of twenty-eight dollars per ton on imported steel and gave protection to domestic producers. In 1872, Carnegie, working with American mechanical engineer Alexander Lyman Holley, constructed his first steel mill, named the Edgar Thomson Steel Works. They designed the plant to combine blast furnaces, forges, and rolling and finishing mills in contiguous locations. Process innovations—for example, the open-hearth furnace—increased production speed, enabled the production of a greater variety of steel products, and, with high-speed capacity, reduced costs.

Carnegie's next step was to integrate vertically. He formed a partnership with Henry Clay Frick, who owned vast coal mines near Pittsburgh, as well as a large number of coke ovens—dome-shaped brick ovens that transformed coal into coke, a more purified compound that generated more heat when burned and could withstand higher temperatures. This partnership furthered Carnegie's vertical integration and allowed him to undercut competitors in price.

The low costs at Carnegie Steel also resulted from the hiring of unskilled immigrant labor. In the 1880s, Frick—famous today for his art collection, but infamous to many in the late nineteenth and early twentieth centuries for his opposition to organized labor—became chairman of Carnegie Steel and sought to recruit workers from southern and eastern Europe. These laborers had little to no knowledge of English and were put in makeshift schools that taught them only enough words to follow their foremen's instructions. Any association of workers, or any outside agent coming to organize the Carnegie workforce, was met with violence. The 1892 strike by the Amalgamated Association of Iron and Steel Workers at Carnegie's Homestead Works was quelled by a heavily armed private security force (known as the Pinkertons) and 4,000 soldiers of the state militia. It was a significant setback to efforts to organize steelworkers, and the incident also heightened racial tensions, as many of the strikebreakers were African Americans, who themselves were often barred from union membership.

Food and tobacco

The late nineteenth century saw the rise of companies producing agricultural and perishable products on an unprecedented scale. These companies not only had to organize and coordinate a high volume of continuous output but also had to find ways to develop national and international distribution networks that reached wholesalers and shop owners.

In cigarettes, James Buchanan Duke, of Durham, North Carolina, was an early entrepreneur. When he started in the industry, cigarette sales were negligible. Those who purchased tobacco products were far more likely to smoke cigars and pipes or chew tobacco. In 1884, he bought two machines, designed by James Albert Bonsack, that produced 120,000 cigarettes in ten hours—far surpassing the amount that could be generated by hand rolling. This output, however, was more than the existing demand. Duke realized that his main challenge would be in advertising and distribution.

Duke's ability to build a national distribution network depended on the rise of two other industries—the credit reporting agency (which assessed the reputations of wholesalers and retailers throughout the country) and the advertising agency (which placed ads in regional newspapers), both of which were based in New York City. Accordingly, Duke moved his operation, W. Duke, Sons & Company, to New York. He started building a national sales force and, with associates, established sales offices in other US cities. He also sought marketing agreements with wholesalers and dealers in countries around the globe. Duke tasked salesmen with visiting grocers, tobacco shops, drugstores, and other retail establishments to boost sales. By 1889, he had sales of $4.5 million annually; in that same year, he spent about $800,000 on advertising in an attempt to edge out competitors.

With the market leveling off and competition increasing, Duke consolidated his various enterprises and aimed to gain control of others. In 1890, he made agreements with four competing companies to form the American Tobacco Company, which then produced about 90 percent of the cigarettes in America.

The meatpacking industry was also transformed during this period, with Chicago as the central hub. Its growth depended on the railroad, the telegraph, advances in a bureaucratic organization, and, most crucially, the new technology of refrigeration. Gustavus F. Swift Sr. was a pioneer of the refrigerated railcar that allowed the initially seasonal industry to operate year-round.

Swift began his career at age fourteen, as apprentice to a butcher in his home state of Massachusetts. He soon went into business on his own, slaughtering cattle and selling the meat door to door. In 1875, he relocated his operation to Chicago, realizing that he could save a great deal of money if he butchered animals in Chicago and shipped only the meat eastward (as freight charges were determined by volume). His quest for efficiency also led to the development of a routinized butchering process, in which animal carcasses were suspended from hooks and moved along a "disassembly line" on overhead belts and pulleys.

Like Carnegie, Swift pursued a strategy of vertical integration, bringing together all parts of the industry, from the ownership of cattle to the process of slaughtering, the construction of warehouses, and the maintenance of distribution networks. Apart from productivity and efficiency, however, slaughterhouses also became notorious for their filth and brutal working conditions, as graphically recounted in Upton Sinclair's *The Jungle* (1906).

Competition in the meatpacking industry was fierce. One of Swift's competitors, Philip Danforth Armour, used similar methods to maximize the efficiency of his operation. Armour even hired chemists to find uses for parts of the animals that had been discarded, transforming waste products into soap, glue, upholstery stuffing, and fertilizer. Like other large companies, Swift, too, started to operate internationally. To increase his supply of beef, Swift acquired operations in Argentina in 1907, which was quickly becoming a new center of meat packing.

Entrepreneurs in the meatpacking industry were matched by others who implemented continuous processing machinery to produce vast volumes of output in other types of food. For example, the Kellogg brothers, John Harvey and Will Keith, developed Toasted Corn Flakes in Battle Creek, Michigan, beginning in the late nineteenth century, and the Kellogg Company went on to produce a variety of other breakfast cereals. Other companies that got their start during this period included C. A. Pillsbury and Company (1872), makers of flour and other grains; Campbell's (1869), which produced canned tomatoes, vegetables, and soup; and the H. J. Heinz Company (1869), makers of ketchup and many bottled and canned foods.

Consolidation and antitrust

All of these firms—Standard Oil, Carnegie Steel, American Tobacco, Swift, and Armour—sought to find ways to coordinate and control high-speed output by finding efficiencies in their production and distribution processes. Beginning in the late nineteenth century, they also began to consolidate their industries. In 1902, for instance, Swift, Armour, and other Chicago-area meatpackers formed the National Packing Company, a group known as "Big Five" that began buying up other meat companies.

Finance was essential in forming these large consolidations. Two bankers, in particular, played a role in enabling combinations through formal channels. The first was Andrew Mellon of Pittsburgh, Pennsylvania. The patriarch of the family, Thomas Mellon, emigrated from Ireland to western Pennsylvania as a child. In his autobiography, he recalled being impressed by the level of luxury attained by other recent immigrant families. The father of the neighboring Negley family, he mused, "must have been a man of considerable ability and energy, judging from the estate he accumulated." At age fourteen, Thomas Mellon discovered a "dilapidated copy of the autobiography of Dr. Franklin." The book, he wrote, "delighted me with a wider view of life and inspired me with new ambition—turned my thoughts into new channels." Mellon loved the maxims of Franklin's "Poor Richard" and credited reading the book as the turning point of his life—affirming his entrepreneurial aspirations.

As an adult, Thomas Mellon built a school in his backyard to train his sons, several of whom went into business. Andrew Mellon and his brother Richard acted as venture capitalists and lent money to entrepreneurs to help found companies, including Gulf Oil, Koppers Chemical, Carborundum Corporation, and the giant aluminum company Alcoa. They also founded the Union Trust Company to manage these growing businesses. The Mellon family soon held a substantial interest in all of the region's major industries, including coal, steel, aluminum, natural gas, construction, railroads, and chemicals.

In consolidating industries, Mellon was surpassed only by J. P. Morgan of New York, who reorganized industrial concerns including General Electric, American Telephone and Telegraph, and International Harvester. In 1901, Carnegie sold his company to J. P. Morgan's new organization, United States Steel Corporation, a conglomerate with many subsidiaries that became the nation's first billion-dollar company in assets, a significant milestone. After the formation of U.S. Steel, privately held industrial firms became rare (except Ford Motor Company) as more and more large companies formed public corporations.

Criticism of big business—especially the extent of its power and influence—was expressed vibrantly in the 1880s by journalists who came to be known as *muckrakers*. (The moniker was a reference to John Bunyan's seventeenth-century allegory *Pilgrim's Progress*, as used pejoratively by Theodore Roosevelt in a speech in 1906.) *McClure's Magazine*, a monthly publication founded in 1893 by a handful of graduates from the Illinois-based Knox College, became the epicenter of such writing. "Big business" was frequently portrayed as an enemy of democratic governance because wealthy titans of industry exercised undue influence over policymakers. Lincoln Steffens, who wrote about corruption in city governments in *McClure's*, reasoned, "In a country where business is dominant, business men must and will corrupt a government." Ida Tarbell, who wrote *History of Standard Oil* in 1904, also concluded that business had become synonymous with immorality and corruption in America: "Very often people who admit the facts, who are willing to see that Mr. Rockefeller has employed force and fraud to secure his ends, justify him by declaring, 'It's business.' That is, 'it's business' has come to be a legitimate excuse for hard dealing, sly tricks, special privileges." Historians and literary critics began to refer to the late nineteenth century as the "Gilded Age," in which a small, but conspicuous wealthy class masked widespread poverty.

Alongside the muckrakers' work to expose corporate misdeeds, there were legislative and judicial efforts to dismantle large corporations found guilty of deliberately restraining trade— whether by price fixing, limiting output, or otherwise diminishing competition. The Sherman Antitrust Act of 1890 prohibited anticompetitive agreements and other efforts by companies to monopolize their respective industries.

During his presidency, Theodore Roosevelt formed a Bureau of Corporations to investigate monopolistic behavior. In 1902, the Roosevelt administration began investigating the "Beef Trust," the organization of the nation's largest meatpackers, for price fixing and dividing the market between a handful of big companies. In the subsequent ruling of *Swift & Co. v. United States* (1905), the

5. A 1905 cartoon from *Puck* magazine suggests the influence American titans of industry had come to have on US policy. Here they are depicted in an imaginary cabinet meeting during the administration of Theodore Roosevelt. John D. Rockefeller appears as secretary of the Treasury, J. P. Morgan as secretary of the Navy, Andrew Carnegie as secretary of state, and, as postmistress general, investor Hetty Green, whose family had made a fortune in whaling.

Supreme Court ruled that Swift and its allies had violated antitrust laws.

Other similar court decisions followed. In 1911, the Supreme Court ruled Standard Oil had violated the Sherman Antitrust Act for its involvement in anticompetitive agreements and other efforts to exert monopolistic control over the oil market. The court found that the company received preferential rates from the railroads, controlled pipelines, and engaged in price cutting to push out competitors. As a result, Standard was broken up into thirty-four independent companies, including present-day ExxonMobil and Chevron. On the same day, in *United States v. American Tobacco Company* (1911), the Supreme Court compelled the American Tobacco Company to dissolve and form several smaller companies, including R. J. Reynolds, Liggett & Myers, and Lorillard. These rulings were emblematic of a new period of antitrust regulation, which—though it did not end the subsequent growth of big business—represented a meaningful development in evolving business–government relations in the early twentieth century.

In part as a reaction to this, companies began to think carefully about what became known as corporate public relations. Companies sought, in effect, to create a "corporate soul"—that is, an explanation of the corporation's purpose and mission to policymakers, society, and its employees. Such a strategy of public relations became one more step in the formation of the modern corporation.

Chapter 6
Modern companies, 1910–1930

By 1917, American industrial firms were among the largest business organizations in the world. Some of the biggest firms were U.S. Steel ($2.45 billion in assets), Standard Oil ($574 million), Bethlehem Steel ($381 million), Armour & Co. ($314 million), and Swift & Co. ($306 million). Cities were dense networks of small and medium-sized firms. In New York City alone, some 32,590 manufacturing establishments employed more than 630,000 wage earners in 1922.

The rapid spread of two new sources of power, electricity and the internal combustion engine, brought significant changes to business and society. Communication technology also improved. Telephone service became more extensive and operated with improved signal capacity and switching functions. Some historians have commented that these new sources of power and communication led to a "second industrial revolution"—just as water power, steam, and coal had launched the "first industrial revolution" a century earlier.

In part as a result of rising disposable income, many of the innovations in this period were intended for consumers as well as for use by businesses. These included appliances for the home, communication and entertainment technologies (such as radio and movies), the automobile, and ready-to-wear clothing.

Simultaneously, businesses in many consumer-oriented lines began investing more in advertising, salesmanship, and promotion.

Door-to-door selling became a popular distribution strategy for some smaller consumer products. In 1892, after many years of selling books and perfume, David H. McConnell started the California Perfume Company, which sold toilet waters, powder, perfumes, and cosmetics and came to rely mostly on women as sales agents. The company changed its name to Avon in the 1930s. In 1906, Alfred C. Fuller organized the Fuller Brush Company to sell brooms, dusters, hairbrushes, and similar items. Like many door-to-door companies, Fuller Brush faced the problem of high employee turnover, as salesmen left the occupation because of the frequent rejections they faced from customers. In response, one salesman for the company, Albert Teetsel, introduced the "Fine and Dandy" club to stimulate positive thinking among employees.

Industrial insurance companies (which sold policies door to door) likewise built large sales forces. In 1898, John C. Merrick, a former slave, founded the North Carolina Mutual Life Insurance Company in Durham, North Carolina. The company provided "burial insurance," which required the collection of nickel or dime weekly premiums by salesmen and was purchased to ensure policyholders a respectable funeral. It grew to become the largest African American company in the country and an anchor for banks and competing insurance companies, also run by African Americans, in Durham. C. C. Spaulding, who led the company in the 1920s, helped promote associations of African American businesspeople, such as the National Negro Insurance Association and the National Negro Business League, which was founded by Booker T. Washington.

The success of individuals like Merrick, Spaulding, and others was set against a backdrop of deep racial divisions and growing Jim Crow segregation that made doing business extraordinarily difficult and often dangerous for African Americans. Still, this period would later be described as the "golden age" of black business in part because of the success of these financial institutions.

The rise of management

One of the most significant changes to business administration during this period was the growing professionalization of management. What began as a pragmatic organizational role within large railroad companies increasingly became a career unto itself.

As companies begin to hire managers to run their sprawling operations, machine makers produced a range of new devices to enhance office efficiency. In 1886, William S. Burroughs (great-grandfather to the Beat writer of the same name) created the American Arithmometer Company and produced one of the first adding machines. In 1905, the company claimed that its device was used by more than 22,000 companies, including banks, department stores, and railroads. Around the same time that Burroughs got his start, E. Remington and Sons, a maker of firearms, became an early manufacturer of another new business machine—the typewriter. In 1878, Remington started to produce typewriters using the QWERTY keyboard. In 1887, the A. B. Dick Company produced the Model 0 Flatbed Duplicator, a mimeograph machine that made multiple copies of documents.

In 1911, Frederick Winslow Taylor published *The Principles of Scientific Management*, which sought to improve factory workflows through greater managerial oversight and close observation and analysis of individual work routines. In one well-known (and often ridiculed) example, Taylor recounted getting one worker, the fictional "Schmidt," at the Bethlehem Steel Company to load pig iron more quickly by giving him some "rough" talk to find out whether he was a "high-priced man" and by having a supervisor with a stopwatch give him detailed instructions: "Now pick up a pig and walk. Now sit down and rest." Still, the management scholar Peter Drucker wrote that Taylor was "the first person in history who did not take work for granted, but looked at it and studied it."

In addition, a range of tools for managerial analysis emerged to facilitate the operation of large corporations. During the 1900s and 1910s, DuPont introduced the concept of return on investment, which allowed managers to more effectively evaluate and compare the success of their investments. Around the same time, industrial psychologists Walter Dill Scott and Hugo Münsterberg designed the first "mental activity" tests to select candidates for jobs. The advent of such methods helped to create the basis for personnel departments.

To train this new managerial class, several colleges and universities, including the University of Pennsylvania, New York University, and Dartmouth, founded business schools. Harvard Business School (founded in 1908) came to be known, in part, for teaching management principles from "case studies" that asked students to wrestle with real-world business problems. Publishers, too, catered to managers by developing a raft of business magazines, such as *Forbes*, *System*, and *Business Week*.

Automobiles

The automobile industry, which became the largest industry in America, got its start in Europe. In 1885, German engineer Karl Benz patented a gasoline-powered car with a single-cylinder engine. In the 1900s and 1910s, new automobile technologies were introduced in the United States by hundreds of producers experimenting not only with gasoline engines but also with steam, electricity, and gas–electric hybrids.

Initially, many entrepreneurs competed to bring a product to market. In 1893, for instance, Charles and Frank Duryea founded the Duryea Motor Wagon Company, the first automobile manufacturing company in the United States. Eight years later, Ransom E. Olds started the Olds Motor Vehicle Company, later known as Oldsmobile, in Lansing, Michigan. There was also the Thomas B. Jeffery Company, which produced the popular Rambler in Kenosha, Wisconsin.

Soon, however, Henry Ford came to dominate the competition. Born in Michigan in 1863, Ford was a machinist who had worked on steam engines for Westinghouse early in his career. His dream, however, was to "put America on wheels." In 1900, this seemed more like pure fantasy than an achievable end: there were few paved roads, horses were the primary method of travel, and cars were still clunky and expensive. In 1901, Ford launched an automobile company with C. Harold Wills, but left after only a year because of disagreements. The next year, Ford, who liked to race cars, established a second automobile manufacturing company, this time with coal dealer Alexander Y. Malcomson, called Ford & Malcomson, Ltd. The company contracted its initial manufacturing to the Dodge brothers, who eventually became investors in the reincorporated Ford Motor Company in 1903.

The same year, Ford introduced the Model A. The car had functional problems, however, and was followed by model after model until Ford hit on the successful Model T. He then began large-scale production in his factory outside Detroit and over time reorganized the factory floor to improve efficiency, using unskilled workers to perform specific repetitive tasks. Ford described the process of creating the moving assembly line as being inspired by the "disassembly line" he observed in meatpacking firms.

Ford's goal was to own and control as much of the entire production process as possible—and to grow as big as possible. To do this, Ford began to acquire businesses spanning the entire supply chain, from timberlands and rubber plantations to iron ore mines and glassworks. By contrast, Ford paid little attention to marketing and relied on a distribution system led by engaging bicycle retailers and others who were tasked with selling the Model T. Together, these strategies proved remarkably successful at reducing costs. The price of the Model T dropped from $850 in 1908 to $290 by 1924. By the time production of the Model T stopped in 1927, Ford had produced 15 million of them.

Ford's Model T became the quintessential standardized product of the twentieth century. A friend noted of Ford, "Standardization was his hobby." In his autobiography, Ford was philosophical on the subject: "Machine production in this country has diversified our life, has given a wider choice of articles than was ever before thought possible—and has provided the means wherewith the people may buy them. . . . Standardization, instead of making for sameness, has introduced unheard-of variety into our life." Ford might have also noted that standardized products could be endlessly altered by users—such as was the case of his Model T, which became popular with associations of tinkerers who shared news of ways to customize Ford's design.

At the same time, Ford—flush with profits—made the unprecedented decision to more than double the minimum wage for his employees. In 1914, he introduced the five-dollar workday, while simultaneously decreasing the length of the day from nine hours to eight. The *New York Times* described this decision as "one of the most remarkable business moves of [Ford's] entire remarkable career." In explanation, Ford treasurer James Couzens said, "We want those who have helped us to produce this great institution and are helping to maintain it to share our prosperity." The ability to offer competitive pay and work hours pushed down the Ford factory's turnover rate, which had always been high, and people flocked from all over to work there. (Not long after, in 1916, President Wilson signed the Adamson Act, which federally mandated the eight-hour workday.)

Ford was the subject of countless newspaper articles and tributes documenting his dazzling success. He became an icon, despite his personal flaws. He was himself virulently anti-Semitic and could also be very naive. For example, he dispatched his own "Peace Ship" to Europe in 1915, thinking himself capable of negotiating an end to World War I. Then, in 1927, he set out to open a rubber plantation in Brazil, complete with an American-style settlement for workers. Fordlandia, as it was known, featured golf courses, ice cream parlors, schools, restaurants, and more, but only lasted a few years.

By 1920, Ford had achieved his goal of selling affordable cars to Americans and, through the export-oriented Ford Motor Company of Canada, to other customers around the world. By then, however, many Americans owned cars, and there was even a market for used autos, which could sell for less than the price of a new Model T. Some customers, moreover, were in the market for a more expensive vehicle and wanted to trade up. The problem for Ford was that when Americans traded up, they often bought vehicles from Ford's rivals.

General Motors

General Motors (GM) had a different origin than Ford, a different understanding of the marketplace, and a different organizational structure. Unlike the Ford Motor Company, GM was a publicly held corporation brought together in 1908 by William Crapo Durant, a colorful stock market investor who had little interest in the day-to-day operations of the business. Pierre du Pont began purchasing GM stock in 1914 and, after World War I, persuaded his family's company, DuPont, to invest $25 million in the firm.

In 1923, DuPont executives installed Alfred P. Sloan as president of GM. A graduate of the Massachusetts Institute of Technology, Sloan, then in his late forties, had spent much of his early career at Hyatt Roller Bearing, a maker of ball bearings that was then partly owned by his father. DuPont executives also implemented a new form of corporate organization at GM, the multidivisional structure, with several autonomous units. DuPont had pioneered this "M-Form" in its businesses during World War I, when it was producing large quantities of munitions—over 1 million pounds a day—for the Allied Powers.

Sloan oversaw the implementation of the M-Form structure at GM. Instead of offering one model, like Ford, GM offered five—in Sloan's words, "one for every purse and purpose." The five car brands included Chevrolet (the low-priced model), Pontiac, Buick, Oldsmobile, and Cadillac (the high-end model). To accurately track performance in each of these product lines, GM implemented separate divisions for each car brand, linking them all with an executive and financial team at the top. GM also had divisions for trucks, parts, and accessories.

Thus, whereas Ford sent his orders down throughout his company, in the multidivisional form at GM, information flowed upward from the division heads to the executives. It allowed company leaders at the very top of the organization to see clearly which divisions were succeeding and which were not so that they could respond and allocate resources accordingly. This transformation proved to be a revolution in aligning the strategy of businesses (cars for different price categories) and the structure of the company (separate divisions for each car brand).

The M-Form became the standard for American companies operating in several different product lines (such as Standard Oil of New Jersey) and those working across many different regions (like Sears Roebuck, in which each region was its own division). It also became influential in Europe, especially after World War II, when American consultants from McKinsey & Company promoted its virtues to European companies that were rebuilding in the late 1940s and 1950s.

As an individual, Sloan—although less well known today than Ford—was equally influential. Sloan's market-oriented approach represented a shift in business strategy, from competing on price and production efficiency (as at Ford) to competing for leadership in market segments by promoting brand names (as at GM). He built a national dealer network and sales organization and created the General Motors Acceptance Corporation to offer loans to GM customers. He also introduced annual models, colors, and variety. Sloan himself said, "It is not too much to say that the 'laws' of the Paris dressmakers have come to be a factor in the automobile industry—and woe to the company which ignores them."

General Motors surpassed Ford in domestic market share in the 1930s and from then on consistently outperformed its competitor in both sales and market share. (GM was the biggest carmaker, in terms of unit sales, in the world before losing the title to Toyota in 1980.) It also outperformed the other of the "Big Three" companies, Chrysler, which was founded by former Buick head Walter Chrysler in 1925 from the remains of the failing Maxwell automobile company.

In the early twentieth century, the automobile industry, centered in Detroit, became so large that it spurred parallel growth in auxiliary sectors like glass, oil, steel, and rubber. For example, the city of Akron, Ohio, became the tire capital of the world, home to the Goodrich Corporation (1870), Goodyear Tire and Rubber Company (1898), Firestone Tire and Rubber (1900), and General Tire (1915).

Marketing

The transition that occurred in the automobile industry—going in stages from many entrepreneurial firms, to one dominant firm (Ford), to a few large competing firms (Ford, GM, and Chrysler) each focusing on specific segments of the consumer market—was emblematic of what historian Richard S. Tedlow defined as the "three phases of marketing."

These three phases provide a constructive lens to understanding the evolution of several other industries, including soft drinks. There were thousands of individual sodas for sale in the late nineteenth century. They began as "tonics," sold by some of the same people who made patent medicines. There were ginger beers, birch beers, sarsaparilla, and a variety of fruit-flavored "mineral waters." In this period, the soft drinks industry could be considered a *fragmented market*.

In 1886, a Georgia pharmacist named John S. Pemberton concocted a mixture of extracts of kola nut and coca leaf with fruit syrup, which he called Coca-Cola. It was initially made with still water. Remarkably, the use of carbonated water started as a mistake when someone pushed the wrong button on the soda fountain and inadvertently gave birth to a global behemoth. Between 1892 and 1903, the Coca-Cola Company spent an astonishing $763,400 on advertising for its new product. The company "unified" the soft drink market by selling Coca-Cola at restaurants, soda fountains, and groceries. It also gave away Coke-branded calendars, glasses, pocket mirrors, pendants, trays, and more. The company allowed individual entrepreneurs to open bottling plants, which created great opportunities for entrepreneurs wanting to enter the industry. Coke dominated the market for decades.

Coke's main competitor, Pepsi-Cola, also got its start in the 1890s, but the company struggled for several decades to get off the ground. Eventually, the company found success by deciding to compete aggressively with Coke on price, offering twice the amount of cola for the same price. Pepsi emerged as a competitor for market share, dividing the cola market just as Ford and GM had divided the automobile market.

Initially, Pepsi sought to segment the market by price alone. However, with postwar inflation in the 1950s, Pepsi could no longer rely solely on low price and came up with a new strategy. In the early 1960s, Pepsi began to advertise its product to younger consumers with a "Pepsi generation" campaign, thereby "segmenting" the marketplace. In response, in 1963 Coca-Cola made several new additions to its product line, each with its own unique packaging and targeted consumer segments. Thus, like the automobile industry, the soda industry transitioned from being fragmented by many companies to being dominated by one company (Coke) and then eventually segmented by brands (including Coke, Pepsi, 7UP, and Dr Pepper).

Electricity

Along with the internal combustion engine (which had a great effect not only on automobiles, but also on tractors and other machines), electricity played a significant role in reshaping American business and society in the 1910s and 1920s. Thomas Edison began experimenting with electricity in the 1870s, testing the idea of providing illumination through an incandescent light bulb. With the support of such financiers as J. P. Morgan and members of the Vanderbilt family, he founded the Edison Illuminating Company and, in 1882, built the first electric generating station in New York City. Later, he created an expanded electric grid for factories. Although Edison was a pioneer, he did not perfect the technology alone: Nikola Tesla, who briefly worked for Edison Machine Works, innovated alternating current as opposed to Edison's direct current.

In factories, electric motors only gradually came to replace those running by water or steam power. However, especially after the 1920s, the effects on manufacturing industries were transformative. For one thing, electric lights and motors allowed factories to run twenty-four hours a day. For another, electricity freed factories of geographic limitations. They no longer had to be near a source of water.

Electricity also had a great impact on urban development during this time. The advent of streetcars, electric power plants, and telephone operating companies changed life in America's great cities, improving everything from transportation to communication, and facilitating ease of construction. Indeed, during this period, the New York City skyline underwent a major transformation with the building of the first skyscrapers. When Western Union constructed its new ten-story headquarters at 195 Broadway in New York City in 1877, it was the tallest building in the country. Many more such imposing structures followed, including the Woolworth Building on 233 Broadway, which opened in 1913. Reaching a height of nearly 800 feet, it was more than three times taller than the Western Union building and is considered one of the first skyscrapers in New York City.

Soon, a range of new consumer electronic appliances began to appear on the market. Several electrical companies, including General Electric and Westinghouse, began to make products, including washing machines, vacuum cleaners, and radios. From 1919 to 1929, the share of homes that had washing machines rose from 8 percent to 29 percent; vacuum cleaners from 4 percent to 20 percent; and radios from 1 percent to 40 percent.

The vacuum cleaner, in particular, became a popular product among American consumers, owned by nearly one-third of households in 1922. One of the first profitable models was manufactured by the Hoover Suction Sweeper Company, named after William Henry Hoover (who purchased the patent for the machine from inventor James Murray Spangler). Hoover introduced the vacuum through advertisements in the *Saturday Evening Post* and offered readers a free ten-day trial. He also sought to develop international markets for the machine in Europe. Hoover sold the machine through retail stores and

6. The Woolworth Building, under construction, photographed in 1912 by Irving Underhill. The nickel-and-dime store founder Frank Woolworth built one of the earliest New York City skyscrapers. The new form of architecture neatly resembled the vertical managerial hierarchy. C. Wright Mills wrote in the 1950s, "Each office within the skyscraper is a segment of the enormous file, a part of the symbol factory that produces the billion slips of paper that gear modern society into its daily shape."

advertised using the slogan "It beats…as it sweeps…as it cleans." One of its competitors, the Eureka Vacuum Company, founded in 1909, started selling its machines door to door, offering homeowners a demonstration, a strategy that put the company in second place, behind Hoover, for much of the 1920s.

The refrigerator was slower to develop but had a much longer history stretching back into the early nineteenth century, when the idea of home refrigeration, using ice blocks, first gained traction. Until 1910, a booming ice industry supplied home iceboxes from Boston to Chicago. One of the first electric refrigerators on the market was the Kelvinator, introduced in 1918 and named in honor of Scottish engineer Lord Kelvin, who discovered the existence of absolute zero. The Frigidaire brand, owned by GM, appeared soon after that. Although early refrigeration ran into numerous challenges and the growth of the industry was slower than for other appliances, electric refrigeration nonetheless revolutionized both purchasing and consumption habits by allowing Americans the ability to safely and easily preserve food.

Not all appliances focused on alleviating housework. Foremost in this category was the radio. In 1919, General Electric entered the industry by establishing the wholly owned subsidiary, the Radio Corporation of America. In the 1920s, the Radio Corporation of America became a major manufacturer of radio receivers and created the National Broadcasting Company. Radio spread much more quickly than did time-saving appliances. In 1930, more than 40 percent of urban Americans had a radio; just ten years later, that number had grown to more than 80 percent.

Part of the appeal of the radio was its immediacy; another was the diversity of news headlines from across the country and around the world. People who could never afford to attend events in person could now listen to made-for-radio operas and even cheer on their favorite sporting teams as they played in real time.

Wall Street

The period from the 1910s to the 1930s also saw the rapid growth of the financial industry and the emergence of a modern financial system. After World War I, New York City became a global financial center, rivaling London, Paris, and Vienna. In 1913, to help avert financial panics, the Federal Reserve System was established, with a board of governors in Washington, DC, and twelve regional banks in different cities—including a powerful branch in New York. Previously, in the nineteenth century, most firms had financed their operations through retained earnings. After the turn of the century, more of them began borrowing from banks and issuing corporate bonds and other financial instruments. Numerous brokerages soon appeared to raise capital for the new enterprises and to fund the expansion of existing ones.

Two leading financial institutions at this time were the "Yankee" firm J. P. Morgan & Co. and Kuhn, Loeb & Co., a firm founded in 1867 by German Jewish immigrant entrepreneur Alexander Kuhn. Kuhn started out his career in the garment industry, manufacturing clothing for the US Army during the Civil War in partnership with his brother-in-law, Solomon Loeb. When the US economy began to grow in the years following the war, the partners entered the financial services industry and soon had built one of the leading investment banks in New York City.

Despite pervasive anti-Semitism, Kuhn, Loeb & Co. frequently collaborated with other leading banks of the time, especially J. P. Morgan, although the two firms never mixed socially. Over the course of several decades, they completed 164 transactions together, worth more than $600 million.

At the same time, investors and bankers in New York had begun to shift their focus from underwriting railroads to financing industrial and public utility companies. The number of industrial stocks listed on the New York Stock Exchange rose from 20 in 1898 to 173 in 1915. Stock ownership increased dramatically as a result of rising per capita wealth and marketing campaigns— including the World War I Liberty Bond drive that introduced many Americans to the idea of owning securities. At the start of the twentieth century, only 500,000 Americans owned stocks (less than 1 percent of the adult population); by the end of the 1920s, that figure had increased to 10 million (about 12 percent).

Increasing stock ownership was also, in part, the result of an improved public understanding of the market. During the 1920s, Wall Street became the focus of an innovative series of financial information services, including Moody's *Manuals*, which analyzed the financial health of thousands of companies and promised to help companies make money by guiding their investments. Along with improved transparency, investment was promoted by the rise of modern economic forecasting. Forecasting newsletters like Roger Babson's *Barometer*, the Harvard Economic Service's newsletter, and Irving Fisher's financial page suggested to investors, bankers, and managers that the trends of prosperity and depression were decipherable. Most of these services simply celebrated the rising stock market of the 1920s and failed to foresee the impending market crash of 1929 and the ensuing Depression. Yale economist Irving Fisher, especially, perhaps the best-known American economist of the early twentieth century, promised in 1929 shortly before the economic collapse in September that American stocks had reached a "permanently high plateau."

Although this optimism would soon be shattered, the economic trends set in place during the early decades of the twentieth century, especially the growth of manager-led capitalism, would come to define the business strategies that lasted for much of the century. Specifically, these strategies included an emphasis on organization and bureaucracy; a view that large companies should be organized as corporations; a belief that companies were best led by professional managers who spent a career in management; and a growing sense that management was a "science," or that it at least benefited from quantitative analysis. Although business had been conducted for millennia without a professional manager class, there now seemed to be no going back—and no going ahead without one.

Chapter 7
Crisis and war, 1930–1945

In the 1930s and 1940s, America's innovative commercial centers—including New York in finance, Pittsburgh in steel, Detroit in automobiles, and Chicago in meatpacking and grain trading—grew to include Washington, DC. Washington's importance to business was not a result of its proximity to natural resources or its manufacturing capacity. Instead, the city's contribution to the development of American industry came from its abundance of planners and policymakers. During these decades, the Great Depression, the New Deal, and World War II fundamentally transformed the American economy into one in which the government played a far bigger role in stimulating, monitoring, guiding, and regulating business. In doing so, politicians and their associates transformed the nature of the relationship between the government (both state and federal) and the economy that had previously existed.

To give one measure of the new "mixed economy" that emerged, federal net outlays (money spent by the US Treasury on specific federal programs with preapproved budgets) increased significantly. In 1929, this figure stood at about 3 percent of the gross domestic product per year. In 1934, during the Great Depression, it grew to 10 percent and then skyrocketed with the onset of World War II to a remarkable 41 percent of the gross domestic product in 1944. (Although federal net outlays fell to 11 percent in 1948, they remained well above pre-Depression levels; in 2020, this figure was about 20 percent of the gross domestic product.)

The Great Depression

Herbert Hoover, who took office on March 4, 1929, was the first self-described "businessman" to assume the presidency. He rose to wealth before World War I, amassing a fortune worth $4 million in a career as a mining engineer and executive. He had keen organizational skills and served as the head of the Commission for Relief in Belgium and the American Relief Administration following World War I. In 1921, he went on to serve as the US secretary of commerce and remained in that position until 1928, when he began campaigning for the presidency. In a speech that year, Hoover pointed to the booming economy and announced the possibility that "poverty will be banished from this nation."

But there were signs of economic trouble amid the prosperity of the 1920s, including falling prices in agriculture and housing and rampant speculation on the stock market. For American farmers, the crisis began in the early 1920s. The demand for agricultural products during World War I was a boon to American farmers, many of whom enlarged their operations in an attempt to meet the seemingly insatiable demand. The price for crops like wheat and corn skyrocketed, leading to a brief period of prosperity. However, when demand decreased after the war, American farmers were left with surplus crops, falling prices, expensive machinery, and often significant debt.

The woes of America's farmers were soon felt in other sectors across the country. On September 3, 1929, the Dow Jones Industrial Average hit a high of 381 but soon began to falter. Sell-offs occurred on October 28 ("Black Monday") and 29 ("Black Tuesday") and the Dow Jones Industrial Average fell sharply from 300 to 230. (In summer 1932 it was at its low point, 41.)

The "Great Crash" of the stock market in October 1929 was a watershed moment for American business. Though the crash did not cause the ensuing depression, it did reveal the fragility of the underlying American financial economy. This raised alarm in both the domestic and the international economies, which were closely tied, especially following World War I when the United States emerged as a creditor country (rather than a debtor, as it had been before).

One hard-hit area was banking. In the 1920s, the American banking system consisted of small banks with limited capital that served only a local community. Rural banks, in particular, had come under pressure as the American population became increasingly urban and as chain stores competed for customers against local shops. Rural banks, already strained, were thus hit especially hard in the early years of the Great Depression. After the dramatic stock market crash, Americans, anxious about the security of their savings, caused a spate of "bank runs" by suddenly and simultaneously withdrawing the entirety of their savings. Between 1930 and 1933, some 9,000 banks (nearly 30 percent of all banks) failed, and many depositors who had not withdrawn their money, in a time without federal insurance, lost their savings.

Like many of his contemporaries, including his Treasury secretary, Andrew Mellon, Hoover initially believed the economy would right itself without direct federal intervention. This belief was rooted in his ideas of American individualism and his faith in voluntary collective action toward the common good. Accordingly, he initially took a conservative approach to the downturn. He gathered business and labor leaders in Washington and implored them not to call for work stoppages and not to cut wages. He also pushed railroad leaders to engage in construction and maintenance, and he proposed that farmers form cooperatives to minimize surplus crops and keep wages high and prices up, but to no avail. Unemployment increased from 15 percent in mid-1931 to 23 percent by early 1932.

By then, the situation had deteriorated to such an extent that Hoover decided to intervene more directly in the economy. He authorized the creation of the Reconstruction Finance Corporation to provide loans to railroads, financial institutions, and local governments. However, it failed to make a significant improvement. On the eve of the presidential election of 1932, Hoover's popularity waned in the face of worsening economic conditions across the country. He was no match for Democratic challenger Franklin Delano Roosevelt, who easily defeated him in a landslide election in November of that year.

The New Deal

Roosevelt ran on a platform of a "New Deal" for the American people. Ahead of his presidential campaign, he assembled a group of advisors and academics, sometimes called his Brain Trust, to develop his policy agenda. The result was a platform characterized by a spirit of pragmatic policy experimentation that addressed banking, business, and labor in the United States.

Within days after his inauguration on March 4, 1933, Roosevelt was meeting with advisors and cabinet members, working to restore confidence in banks and encourage Americans to redeposit their savings. On March 6, he declared a "bank holiday" that shut down the entire banking system to prevent further bank runs. Three days later, Roosevelt sent Congress the Emergency Banking Act, designed to stabilize, strengthen, and reopen solvent banks.

Roosevelt was aware of the need to reassure the public of the security of the nation's banks before the banks could reopen. On March 12, he broadcast a "fireside chat"—the first of many radio addresses throughout his presidency to discuss the causes of the banking crisis and outline his administration's plan to address it.

The next day, Monday, March 13, the twelve Federal Reserve Banks reopened. In just three days, 70 percent of banks (more than 12,000 institutions) had reopened. By April, another 1,300 banks were back in business and Americans had redeposited more than two-thirds of the currency withdrawn during the crisis. As Roosevelt's advisor Raymond Moley later reflected, "capitalism was saved in eight days."

After the successful implementation of the Emergency Banking Act, Roosevelt set about developing a long-term solution to prevent a similar crisis from occurring in the future. Initially, Roosevelt had been skeptical of enacting a sweeping legislative reform program, but he found widespread support for reform from both Democrats in Congress and the public, especially following federal investigations of the banking industry. The Pecora Commission—a body formed in 1932 to investigate the causes of the 1929 stock market crash—provided a wealth of detail on how banks and other financial institutions abused power, misled investors, and provided insider advantages. Such findings, along with the publication of scathing accounts of the business elite, like Harvey O'Connor's *Mellon's Millions* (1933) and Matthew Josephson's *Robber Barons: The Great American Capitalists, 1861-1901* (1934), intensified public outrage against business and financial leaders.

In response to this call for reform, Congress passed the Banking Act of 1933. The legislation had many features, including what became known as the Glass–Steagall Act, which separated commercial and investment banks. Glass–Steagall prevented securities firms and investment banks from taking deposits and stopped Federal Reserve member banks from underwriting or distributing nongovernmental securities. Significantly, the Banking Act also established the Federal Deposit Insurance Corporation, which introduced deposit insurance in US commercial banks and savings institutions. The initial plan insured deposits for up to $2,500. In 1935, the Federal Deposit

Insurance Corporation became a permanent agency of the government, and the insurance limit rose to cover balances up to $5,000.

In addition, Roosevelt sought to improve the transparency of financial markets. The Securities Act of 1933 required financial reports from public corporations—mandating the disclosure of balance sheets, profit-and-loss statements, and the names and compensation of corporate officers. The following year, the US Securities and Exchange Commission was established to regulate the stock market. The introduction of new financial and securities legislation during this period, necessitating increased government oversight and review of financial statements, contributed to the growth of the accounting profession and management consulting.

Public works and infrastructure

In 1933, Roosevelt launched a series of programs aimed at improving public works and infrastructure, which also had positive implications for commerce. For example, he began a major building initiative through the Works Progress Administration and Public Works Administration, which built thousands of schools, libraries, hospitals, public office buildings, and new roads and even undertook larger projects like the construction of LaGuardia Airport and the Lincoln Tunnel in New York City. Roosevelt also supported the Tennessee Valley Authority Act, which chartered a federally owned corporation to provide energy, flood control, fertilizer manufacturing, and other services to promote economic development in the rural Tennessee Valley. The Tennessee Valley Authority represented a milestone for development in that region, which was previously largely without access to electricity and other modern conveniences enjoyed by many urban Americans. Finally, Roosevelt founded the Civilian Conservation Corps, a group that employed young men (typically between the ages of eighteen and twenty-five) to work toward the development and conservation of rural land.

The New Deal also aimed at regulating business directly and improving the lives of America's working class. The National Industrial Recovery Act called on business leaders to accept a minimum wage and maximum hours and to abolish child labor. It brought together business representatives from many industries to design codes and standards for their respective industries. The National Labor Relations Act of 1935 gave employees the right to join unions and compelled companies to bargain in good faith with union leaders. This agreement contributed to significant growth in union membership during this period, particularly for the American Federation of Labor and the Congress of Industrial Organizations. Unions won concessions from auto manufacturers, lumber companies, and mine owners. Americans also benefitted from the 1935 Social Security Act, which established a system of universal retirement pensions, unemployment insurance, and welfare benefits.

Roosevelt, and his programs, proved highly popular with the American people, who re-elected him in 1936, 1940, and 1944. However, the president also had critics. Many business leaders, including Pierre du Pont, opposed New Deal policies, which they viewed as invasive, especially the requirement for publicly traded companies to report their financial health. The National Association of Manufactures (founded in 1895) and the Liberty League (founded directly in response to the New Deal in 1934) were vocal opponents of Roosevelt's agenda, protesting what they perceived as the antibusiness radicalism of the New Deal. The proliferation of oppositional sentiment during this period was a key element in the development of the modern conservative movement, in which businesses came to see themselves in opposition to the government.

The New Deal also faced opposition in the courts. In 1935, the Supreme Court challenged the constitutionality of the National Industrial Recovery Act in the case *Schechter Poultry Corporation v. United States*. The Brooklyn butchery was charged with violations of new federal codes instituted under the New Deal—including the sale of an "unfit chicken"—and the company sued on the grounds that the National Industrial Recovery Act represented an unconstitutional delegation of legislative authority to the executive branch. The Supreme Court agreed, writing a unanimous opinion in favor of Schechter. In 1937, Roosevelt also failed in his effort—commonly referred to as the "court-packing plan"—to add justices to the Supreme Court (one for every member over the age of seventy) to help gain more favorable rulings for his programs.

Despite experiencing some setbacks, the New Deal transformed the business landscape. Many of its provisions have remained vital for decades afterward, including the Federal Deposit Insurance Corporation, Social Security, and the National Labor Relations Board. The regulation of the banking and securities industries, in particular, laid the foundation for decades of productive economic growth—not only during the 1940s, but also through much of the rest of the century. Moreover, the approach Roosevelt took—launching large federal projects and deficit spending during periods of deep recession and depression—became emblematic of a new approach to economic policy embodied in John Maynard Keynes's *General Theory* (1936). Keynes had been promoting the idea of deficit spending to combat depression for over a decade. Indeed, even before Roosevelt assumed the presidency, Keynes wrote to him with advice on how to end the crisis in the United States. Although the extent to which Keynes influenced Roosevelt's policy agenda is unclear, many New Dealers and the next generation of academic economists became committed Keynesians.

Innovation

Despite the economic setback caused by the Depression, not all companies suffered equally. People still needed to buy food, soap, and other items necessary for daily existence. They also continued to seek entertainment, paying twenty cents per ticket to go to the movies. Indeed, American film companies, such as Paramount Pictures and Metro-Goldwyn-Mayer, produced a considerable number of movies—about 5,000—during the 1930s. Most were forgettable, but some endured as classics, including *Duck Soup* (1933), *It Happened One Night* (1934), *Snow White and the Seven Dwarfs* (1937), and *The Wizard of Oz* (1939).

Despite massive corporate cuts in investment during the 1930s, firms continued their commitment to innovation that had begun in the 1920s with the founding, for example, of Western Electric and AT&T's Bell Labs in 1925. Between 1929 and 1936—the worst years of the Depression—an average of seventy-three corporate labs were founded per year.

Between 1933 and 1940, the number of employees in research and development divisions of US manufacturing companies grew from about 11,000 to 28,000. These labs produced many new products, including synthetic fabrics from DuPont, improvements in radio at Zenith, and, at Westinghouse and the Radio Corporation of America, innovations that would lead to television. New companies also emerged during this period, including Geophysical Service, Inc. (1931), which later became Texas Instruments, and Hewlett–Packard (1939).

One company that experienced growth during this period was IBM, under the leadership of Thomas J. Watson Sr., a former salesman and manager who had trained under John H. Patterson at National Cash Register, a company renowned for its systematic approach to salesmanship. IBM was a highly diversified company that sold many different business machines, but Watson focused his energy on improving the company's information-processing capacities. The ability to quickly sort through volumes of stored data made IBM's equipment invaluable following the passage of the National Recovery Act in 1933 and the Social Security Act of 1935—both of which created an unprecedented demand for storing data. Sure enough, the US government soon became IBM's biggest client. As Watson's son, Thomas J. Watson Jr., would later recall, "the vital statistics of the whole country went onto punch cards."

War production

During the New Deal, the economy slowly improved, except for a downturn in 1937–38. But the New Deal programs did not end the Great Depression. Only spending for World War II did that. After the German invasion of Poland in 1939 that started the war, more than 16 million Americans would serve in the US armed forces during the conflict. The government built factories, funded the reorganization of existing plants, and purchased artillery, machines, and weapons at unprecedented levels. By 1945, the United States had spent some $315.8 billion on mobilization.

However, at the outset of the war in Europe, public opinion in the United States was strongly isolationist. Congress passed three neutrality acts from 1935 to 1937, forbidding the shipment of arms to foreign combatants and prohibiting loans to belligerents. Roosevelt, though, was convinced that the United States needed to ready itself for war by building up its military and increasing productive capacity to assist the Allies in the supply of munitions and machinery.

Indeed, the Allies' need for armaments was dire. In May 1940, Germany launched an effective blitzkrieg against Belgium, the Netherlands, and France. With the British evacuation at Dunkirk in late May and early June 1940, the British army abandoned nearly 700 tanks, 11,000 machine guns, 850 antitank guns, some 65,000 cars, trucks, and motorcycles, and much more.

At the time, the United States did not have a ready supply of military equipment or the infrastructure in place to produce it. The fledgling US munitions industry of World War I had either been dismantled or collapsed as a result of low demand after the armistice. Bethlehem Steel, for instance, had smashed its unused war machinery into scrap metal. Even the shipbuilding industry, which had been somewhat revived by the 1936 Merchant Marine Act, struggled to keep pace with demand from the British navy. Before producers were able to consider building airplane engines, tanks, or ships, the entire machine tool industry had to be rebuilt. Donald Nelson, a Sears executive chosen to head the Office of Production Management (1941–42) and the War Production Board (1942–44), recalled, "There were hardly enough tanks to fight a regiment of well-armed Boy Scouts. There were few small arms, and almost no ammunition."

Existing factories also needed to be overhauled. Recalled GM president and chief executive officer Alfred Sloan, "When we were mobilized during World War II, we were obliged to transform the great bulk of our operations almost completely, to learn rapidly and under great pressure how to produce tanks, machine guns, aircraft propellers, and many other kinds of equipment with which we had no experience at all." This required the training of many thousands of workers.

The American war effort was possible only thanks to the government-led coordination of thousands of US firms, which worked collectively to mobilize American industry. Still, there were delays and bottlenecks in every sector and the flow of raw materials was challenging to prioritize, or ration. To aid in this effort, in 1941 Nelson recruited Wall Street lawyer Ferdinand Eberstadt to serve as chairman of the Army and Navy Munitions Board. In this role, Eberstadt allocated steel, aluminum, and copper to different industries through a bidding process, so that the government could ensure that each element of the war production industry had access to an adequate supply of materials.

Because of the widespread enlistment of men, women performed much of the work of mobilization—finding employment at hundreds of factories and businesses across the country. Indeed, some 5 million women joined the US workforce between 1940 and 1945. By 1945, women accounted for 37 percent of the workforce. Many found work in the defense plants, building tanks, airplane engines, and trucks, as well as at companies like Standard Oil, where women performed complex chemical work.

African Americans also played a major role in wartime industrial production. A. Philip Randolph and other African American labor rights activists eventually persuaded President Roosevelt to issue Executive Order 8802 (1941), which banned discrimination in the defense industries. The Fair Employment Practices Committee was formed in the same year to ensure the implementation of the order. Randolph and others continued to press for racial equality during and after the war, ultimately leading President Harry Truman to issue Executive Order 9981 in 1948, ending segregation in the armed services.

Among the largest contracts to build US war machinery were $2.9 billion to Ford to produce airplane engines, $2.6 billion to Chrysler to manufacture tanks and trucks, and $2.5 billion to Lockheed Aircraft Company to build airplanes. Indeed, during the war, the aircraft industry grew tremendously—from producing 5,900 planes in 1939 to an astonishing 95,300 in 1944, the year of highest production. This rate far outpaced that of any other country. Growth also brought innovation in aircraft engine design, the introduction of jet power, and the development of high-octane aviation fuel. Boeing Aircraft, founded in 1916, was well positioned to take advantage of demand and experienced significant growth during the war. Boeing would go on to produce two of the most successful bombers, the B-17 (the Flying Fortress) in the 1930s and, toward the end of the war, the B-29 (the Superfortress).

The automobile industry played a central role in mobilization efforts. The industry was more than a few large firms clustered in Detroit. If one counted all the manufacturers of die tools and subcontractors who built parts and gadgets for cars, Donald Nelson said, "The industry includes about 1,050 factories, owned by an estimated 850 motor vehicle and parts companies, as well as thousands of subcontractors and suppliers located in 1,375 cities and 44 states." At the beginning of the war, a half million people worked directly for the automobile industry, and 7 million others were indirectly employed. Demand for munitions was such that— in addition to the conversion of existing factories—the government also directly financed the construction of new plants to meet military equipment production targets. Such projects were overseen by the Defense Plant Corporation, a subsidiary of the Reconstruction Finance Corporation founded by Roosevelt in 1940 for expressly this purpose. The Defense Plant Corporation was one of eight wartime subsidiaries founded to further the American war effort, which together undertook everything from infrastructure development, to the construction of new machinery, to the production of synthetic rubber.

Much of this government-led mobilization was handled by businessmen from large firms, along with Nelson and the lawyer Eberstadt. For example, Roosevelt tapped William Knudsen, who successfully headed Chevrolet before succeeding Sloan as president of GM, to lead the National Defense Advisory Commission. In his prior career, Knudsen had been the biggest proponent of "flexible mass production," a process that allowed regular modification and improvement in response to new technology or market demands. Roosevelt also called on Charles E. Wilson, president of General Electric, to serve on the War Production Board in the later years of the war.

Corporations were also deeply involved in the production of the atomic bombs dropped on Hiroshima and Nagasaki in 1945. There were three major sites involved in producing the weapons: Site W in Hanford, Washington, where DuPont created factories to produce plutonium; Site X in Oak Ridge, Tennessee, where representatives from Eastman Kodak and Union Carbide oversaw two large facilities dedicated to enriching uranium; and Site Y in Los Alamos, New Mexico, where scientists designed, assembled, and built the bombs. Oak Ridge sprawled over 59,000 acres of sparsely settled land twenty miles west of Knoxville, Tennessee, and employed a construction force of 20,000 workers to build the complex. "You see, I told you it couldn't be done without turning the whole country into a factory," observed the physicist Niels Bohr, visiting Los Alamos, to colleague Edward Teller: "You have done just that."

Reconversion

By the end of the war, the total wartime output of American factories exceeded Roosevelt's initial estimates. Manufacturers had produced 456,000 aircraft engines, 86,000 tanks, 600,000 jeeps, 2 million trucks, 17 million guns, 193,000 artillery pieces, and 41 billion rounds of ammunition. Shipyards in California alone had launched 12,000 warships and merchant ships and 65,000 smaller boats and landing craft.

As Nelson recalled, "By the beginning of 1945, planes were flying out of Uncle Sam's star-spangled costume like a plague of moths." He attributed the success in mobilization to several factors. The first was standardization and mass production. The United States had developed more advanced, large-scale manufacturing operations than any other country. Second, business leaders in the United States showed a great spirit of cooperation and exchanged patents and different organizational strategies "despite their history of competition." Third, Nelson found that business leaders' competitiveness could be successfully channeled into setting production records. Highly skilled technicians worked with a spirit of constructive and cooperative problem-solving toward national, rather than corporate, goals.

Technology had played a major part in the war in communications, weaponry, medicine, and other fields. The

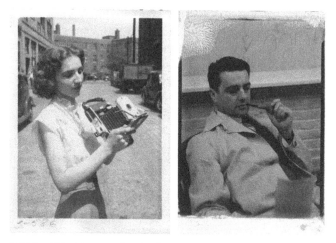

7. Polaroid test images, showing Meroë Marston Morse, a leading scientist at Polaroid who helped develop high-speed black and white films and encouraged famous photographers to use Polaroid cameras; and the company founder, Edwin Land, a pioneer of instant photography and renowned inventor.

British developed electronic computers to break Nazi secret codes and invented radar. Americans, too, built early digital computers. The Electronic Numerical Integrator and Computer (ENIAC), for instance, was completed in 1945. The US Department of Agriculture in Peoria, Illinois, invented a way to mass-produce penicillin.

Some of these innovations found application after the war. Polaroid Corporation, founded in 1937 by Edwin Land to manufacture polarized sunglasses, designed numerous products during the war including infrared glasses for night vision. A few years after the war, the company, located in Cambridge, Massachusetts, introduced instant photography with the Polaroid Camera Model 95.

By 1945, despite rationing and the massive redirection of resources toward war production, American consumers were eating more meat, buying more shoes and gasoline, and using more electricity than they had at the beginning of the war. Americans took home higher wages and were among the most productive workers in the world. As the conversion to a peacetime economy began, production became focused again on homes, appliances, and automobiles.

Chapter 8
Corporate America, 1945–1980

World War II left the nations of Europe devastated. Major cities, including Berlin, Dresden, London, and Vienna, endured massive aerial bombing. The war displaced millions of people from their homes; transportation infrastructure—including roads, bridges, and railroads—was damaged or destroyed. Nearly 36.5 million Europeans, including Russians, died between 1939 and 1945 from war-related causes. Japan was in ruins following the firebombing of Tokyo and the atomic bombing of Hiroshima and Nagasaki. The two atomic bombs alone are estimated to have killed or wounded more than 200,000 people.

By contrast, the United States suffered 418,000 war-related deaths and its infrastructure emerged unscathed, in fact, stronger than it had been before. Its large corporations dominated global markets, its superior military power was unquestioned, and its capacity for technological innovation was unsurpassed.

Indeed, the decades immediately after the war were a golden age for American business. Manufacturers in the United States—located in cities that had escaped aerial bombing—became world leaders in oil, rubber, chemicals, pharmaceuticals, electric equipment, mass-produced machinery, appliances, automobiles, metals, processed foods, drink, and tobacco. In the 1950s, a person seeking to buy a television could choose from more than ten different American brands, including Admiral, Calbest, DuMont, Emerson, Pioneer, and the Radio Corporation of America (RCA). Construction companies also prospered thanks to new growth in the housing market, which had been dormant during the Great Depression and the war. More than a million new housing units were built annually from 1946 to 1955. A testament to this period of prosperity, the US economy grew by an average of 3.8 percent per year from 1946 to 1973.

At the helm of this booming economy were the business executives who had played an essential role in mobilizing American industry during the war. Harley Earl, who had established a wartime camouflage research and training division at GM, became head of GM's car styling team and introduced the wraparound windshield, two-tone paint, tail fins, and many other iconic design features of the low and long cars of the 1950s and 1960s. After serving on the War Production Board, Ralph Cordiner returned to General Electric, serving as president from 1950 to 1958 and as chief executive officer (CEO) from 1958 to 1963, moving the company further into airplane engine building.

Organization men and women

General Electric, DuPont, GM, AT&T, and Westinghouse all extended their research and development activities by building specialized research centers that had remarkable modern glass-and-metal architecture. The Finnish American architect Eero Saarinen designed the GM Technical Center in Warren, Michigan (1956), the IBM Thomas J. Watson Research Center in Yorktown Heights, New York (1961), and Bell Laboratories in Holmdel Township, New Jersey (1962). The federal government also continued to sponsor corporate research, much of it driven by new defense projects for the Cold War. Indeed, the decades after World War II saw the rise of the so-called military–industrial complex, a phrase first articulated by President Eisenhower in his farewell address in 1961 in reference to the growing segment of the economy with a vested economic interested in waging war. In that speech, Eisenhower underscored the importance of America's capacity for military production, yet warned about the potential for the misuse of the immense power that it afforded.

Ironically, during this period of innovation the leadership of large American companies was defined by homogeneity, conformity, and a high degree of corporate loyalty—traits described in sociologist William H. Whyte's *The Organization Man* (1956). Many managers and senior executives worked at the same company, or at least in the same industry, for their entire careers. Whyte's book portrayed a safe "pipeline" running from colleges to recruiting offices and, eventually, to quiet suburban communities. In the 1950s, one college senior quoted in *Organization Man* admitted, "I don't think AT&T is very exciting. But that's the company I'd like to join. If a depression comes there will always be an AT&T."

At the largest firms, senior business leaders were almost uniformly white, male, and Protestant, and the position of "executive" became something of an American archetype. The editors of *Fortune* produced *The Executive Life* (1956) with chapters on "Who are the Executives?," "How Hard Do Executives Work?," "How Executives Crack Up," and "How to Retire Executives."

A remarkable travel service from this period was United Airlines' men-only "Chicago Executive" flights, which operated from 1953 to 1970 with travel between Chicago and New York and Los Angeles to San Francisco. Print advertisements for the Chicago route described the exclusive offering as a "club in the sky" on the Douglas DC-6. Cigar and pipe smoking was permitted, and customers were served cocktails along with a steak dinner.

The postwar business norms of the 1950s encouraged a new, distinct culture and set of values. Those hoping to climb the corporate ladder no longer turned, as Thomas Mellon had, to

Benjamin Franklin's *The Way to Wealth* and its philosophy of dedication, perseverance, and thrift. Now, they looked to the advice of Dale Carnegie's *How to Win Friends and Influence People* (1936), which advocated smiling, getting along, and ingratiating oneself with colleagues and clients as the key to success. Young executives, according to this new thinking, needed "people skills" to navigate corporate bureaucracies. Carnegie's book sold millions of copies in more than thirty languages.

Large businesses grew, overall, increasingly homogenous in their management at the same time as most firms proclaimed, unironically, that they advocated meritocracy in their hiring. Corporate leaders often summed up their firm's values with phrases such as "free competition" and "equality of opportunity," while unhesitatingly dismissing the merit of entire classes of people, most specifically African Americans and women.

Rosabeth Moss Kanter's 1977 book, *Men and Women of the Corporation*, described the consequences of "organization man" homogeneity for talented women. Well into the 1960s and 1970s, women remained unable to break out of gender-segregated roles, mostly clerical and secretarial jobs, to which they were relegated in the 1950s. Those few who did achieve managerial posts faced the problem of tokenism: When they failed, they were seen as representing all women; when they succeeded, they were viewed as exceptions or as possessing masculine characteristics.

In response to these and other obstacles to equal opportunity in the workforce, activists and civil rights leaders began to organize and agitate for fair employment practices. Progress came only intermittently. Indeed, 1964 saw both passage of a major Civil Rights Act (which banned discrimination based on race, color, religion, sex, or national origin and ended racial segregation) and riots in Rochester, New York (the home of Xerox and Eastman Kodak) protesting unemployment among African Americans in that city and discriminatory housing shortages.

Another important development came in the 1970s, when the Equal Employment Opportunity Commission (founded in 1965) gained more power to bring complaints against companies that failed to support and promote diversity. In 1973, a group of female and African American male employees of AT&T tested this new power and won a multi-million-dollar settlement in their suit over discrimination in the workplace. A *Business Week* report from 1975 called the AT&T case "the single strongest influence on corporate employment practices regarding women." Increasingly, for many managers and executives, fear of facing a penalty gradually gave way to a recognition of the intrinsic benefits of employee diversity and the conviction that "fair employment is good business." Still, it was not until the very end of the twentieth century that women started to break into positions of leadership at major firms. In 1999, Carly Fiorina became head of Hewlett–Packard. In 2001, Anne Mulcahy became CEO of the Xerox Corporation; she was succeeded in that position by Ursula Burns, the first African American woman to become head of a Fortune 500 corporation. In 2011, Indra Nooyi was appointed CEO of PepsiCo and Margaret "Meg" Cushing Whitman became head of Hewlett–Packard. But even by 2014, although women accounted for 45 percent of employees in S&P 500 companies, they held only 4.6 percent of CEO positions.

American manufacturing

In 1955, *Fortune* published its first list of the 500 largest companies in the United States, revealing the enormous scale and scope of the American economy. Businesses on the list fell into three broad groups. The first was large manufacturers in industries that made established or "stable technology" products (automobiles, oil, rubber, metals, and other nonelectric machinery). Such businesses typically competed with one another by making minor improvements in their product or in their processes of distribution or production. The second group was manufacturers in "high-tech" industries (such as aviation and chemicals), who competed through the commercialization of new research and development. The final category was manufacturers in "low-tech" goods (including clothes and food), where innovations usually occurred in marketing, branding, and distribution.

Among the firms clustered in established manufacturing industries, GM topped the list with annual revenues of $9.8 billion and a staggering 624,011 employees worldwide. General Motors was the largest company in the country's largest industry. By mid-century, the United States produced 75 percent of the total world automobile output, with Great Britain, the second-largest producer, contributing only about 10 percent.

Ford, under Henry Ford II (grandson of Henry Ford and CEO of the company from 1945 to 1979), rebounded from the difficulties the company had faced in the 1930s—largely by hiring away GM executives and creating a multidivisional structure like its rival. With its new approach, Ford outpaced Chrysler, the third of the "Big Three" companies. The three car companies competed with one another by introducing annual models with an array of stylistic changes, setting high sales quotas for franchisees, and undertaking advertising campaigns in print and on radio and television.

The cars of the 1950s and 1960s tended to be more powerful, wider, and longer than their predecessors. They emphasized style and an abundance of chrome. The 1955 Chevrolet Bel Air (first introduced in 1950) had a V8 engine and featured chrome fenders and chrome spears on the hood. It also had GM's Powerglide automatic transmission. The Cadillac Eldorado was an extreme example of exuberant styling with, in the late 1950s, large vertical tail fins.

Despite new tools for consumer research (including studies by industrial psychologists), carmakers occasionally missed the mark.

8. The Cadillac Eldorado, 1958. The epitome of late-1950s style, parked at Tavern on the Green, New York City. The premium luxury car featured chrome bumpers, a jeweled grille, power seats, a dual four-barrel V8 engine, power windows, air conditioning, glove-box drink tumblers, and tail fins. It was an entirely different conception of the automobile than the simple Volkswagen Beetle, then gaining in popularity.

Ford launched a media blitz to sell the cars of its new Edsel division in the late 1950s. The company spent ten years and over $250 million on the car's development and hoped to create a buzz by hosting a public car-naming contest and spending lavishly on television, print, and radio ads. Still, sales were poor. The car gained a reputation for unreliability and its styling was a significant departure from popular trends of the day. The car featured a horse-collar radiator grille, to evoke nostalgia, and its rear-end, horizontal tail fins. It was an ungainly blend of past and present. The Edsel division lasted from just 1958 to 1960. Overall, however, the automobile industry was so profitable that such failures mattered little. Other models, including the muscle cars such as the Ford Mustang (1964), the Chevrolet Camaro (1966), and the Pontiac Firebird (1967), sold well.

High-tech

A second group of manufacturers focused not on established technologies but on new, innovative high-tech sectors, including aviation, electronics, pharmaceuticals, and petrochemicals. Corporations in these industries competed with one another more often through research and development efforts and by attracting government funding rather than through marketing. Two industries that proliferated during this period were aviation and aerospace. The leading companies were Boeing (Seattle), Douglas Aircraft (Santa Monica), Lockheed and North American Aviation (Los Angeles), General Dynamics and Curtiss–Wright (New York), Martin (Maryland), and American–Marietta (Chicago). In 1955, Boeing had revenues of $1 billion and Douglas Aircraft trailed closely at $900 million.

The largest company in the jet engine industry was GE, which ranked fourth on the Fortune 500 list in 1955, with revenues of $2.9 billion. During World War II, GE transformed itself from an electric systems company to a technology giant that produced turbines, airplane engines, and other complex machines. After the war, the jet engine industry seemed headed for difficulty with impending drops in military demand, but the onset of the Cold War staved off a decline. In 1947, GE produced the J-47 engine, used by the Air Force in its new B-47 bomber, a long-range, six-engine turbojet designed to fly at high speed and high altitude to avoid enemy detection. By 1953, GE manufactured 60 percent of the jet engines built in the United States—nearly all for military use. During this period, GE also began to convert some of its models into commercial aircraft as the company entered the burgeoning business and leisure jet-travel industry.

The postwar period was also one of expansion for the electronics industry, as companies slowly made advances in the development of digital computers. No firm illustrates this postwar surge in innovation better than IBM. Thomas J. Watson Jr., who took over from his father as president of the company in 1952, oversaw a period of growth. In his memoirs, he described his goal of making significant investments in building computers. "That meant hiring engineers by the thousands and spending dollars by the tens of millions for new factories and labs," he wrote; "The risk made Dad balk, even though he sensed the enormous potential of electronics as early as I did."

Watson led the company past computer rivals such as Remington Rand (maker of the popular Univac), GE, NCR, and Burroughs. Among the company's innovations during this period was the computer language FORTRAN, which was quickly adopted by other companies, and the airline reservation system SABRE, which was developed in collaboration with American Airlines and launched in 1964. Before the development of SABRE, American Airlines had been handling all booking and reservations manually—a tedious process that prevented the company from being able to rapidly and cost-effectively scale its operations. In the following years, IBM teamed up with other major airlines to develop similar systems.

IBM's biggest gamble, and its greatest payoff, came from the IBM System/360, an entirely new system of mainframe computers and peripherals that allowed both scientific and commercial users to expand their components and software as their needs grew. The original, announced in 1964 and sold beginning in 1965, could perform an astonishing 34,500 instructions per second. The IBM System/360 was one of the most significant innovations of the period and contributed to the so-called third industrial revolution, which saw the advent of digital computers and the commercialization of information.

Low-tech

Along with high-tech companies, the American manufacturing sector included many low-tech producers, including those in the food, lumber, tobacco, and brewing industries. The meatpacker

Swift (with $2.5 billion in revenues in 1955) was number seven on the Fortune 500 list, and its competitor, Armour (with $2 billion), was number nine. National Dairy Products (a maker of ice cream), General Foods, and Borden were all in the top forty largest firms in the country.

Many of these low-tech companies sought to avoid intense price competition in their respective industries by use of branded products. The breakfast cereal industry—which included such companies as Kellogg's, General Mills, Quaker Oats, and Post— offers a window into the inventive marketing strategies that emerged. To stimulate demand, cereal manufacturers turned to television, a new medium that was becoming increasingly popular. (Although only 9 percent of American households had a television set in 1950, a remarkable 83 percent did by the end of the decade.)

In the early 1950s, Kellogg sponsored its first television show and later hired a Chicago-based advertising agency to create the iconic Tony the Tiger (drawn by Disney animators), which debuted with Frosted Flakes in 1952. By 1958, the four largest cereal-producing companies spent $47 million annually on television promotion. Post advertised its cereals on the *Bugs Bunny Show*; General Mills on *Rocky and His Friends*; and Kellogg's on *The Andy Griffith Show*. This period saw the advent of many cereals that are still popular in the early twenty-first century—including Post's Alpha-Bits (introduced in 1958), Kellogg's Apple Jacks (1965), Quaker Oats' Cap'n Crunch (1963), and General Mills' Lucky Charms (1964), which used the slogan, "They're magically delicious!"

Services

The size of the service sector also grew during the postwar decades, in fast-food restaurants, for instance, as well as healthcare and leisure travel. In 1947, service-industry firms accounted for 46 percent of total US employment. By 1976, that figure had risen to 61 percent.

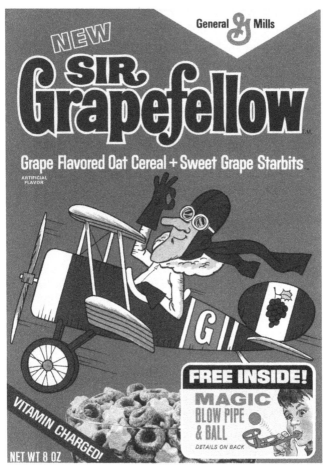

Corporate America, 1945–1980

9. Sir Grapefellow, from General Mills about 1972, was one of many children's cereals introduced in the 1970s through television advertising campaigns. Sir Grapefellow and his nemesis, Baron von Redberry, did not last long, but other cereals with cartoon champions fared better, including the monsters Count Chocula and Frankenberry.

Some service industries grew as "franchises." Franchising had existed in the United States since the nineteenth century. Singer Sewing Machine (in 1850), GM (1898), and Coca-Cola (1899) all relied on building franchises in the early days of their businesses. For example, Coke sold gallons of syrup to individual entrepreneurs, who opened bottling plants and distribution companies to sell Coca-Cola directly to grocers, restaurants, and other outlets. Oil companies also sold franchises to service stations. These "product-oriented" franchises allowed for the recruitment of entrepreneurial individuals to build retail outlets to promote products throughout the country.

A second type of franchising, a "business format" franchise, appeared in the 1920s with the formation of Howard Johnson's restaurants. This type of franchise owner not only sold the franchisor's product but also acquired marketing and management plans and quality-control systems and, in a sense, ran his or her own business. Increasingly, starting in the 1950s, franchising had tremendous appeal to Americans who wanted to start their own businesses but either lacked the start-up capital or wished to avoid some of the risks of founding a business on their own. Business format franchising, especially, became popular at restaurants (such as McDonald's and Kentucky Fried Chicken), hotels, groceries, and auto supply shops. In 1969, there were roughly 380,000 franchises operating in the United States; this figure grew to 440,000 by 1980.

The burger industry became a site of franchise-based competition between White Castle (1921), Jack in the Box (1951), Burger Chef (1954), Burger King (1954), and McDonald's (1955). The McDonald's company grew through franchise ownership and profited, especially, from headquarters' control of franchise real estate. The McDonald brothers founded their restaurant in the 1930s but eventually sold their interest in the firm in 1955 to Ray Kroc, a milk shake–maker salesman. That same year, Kroc started the McDonald's Corporation and reorganized the company.

The new McDonald's provided franchise owners with enough responsibility to give them the feeling of being independent entrepreneurs and allowed them to earn substantial profits, yet McDonald's retained control over menu choices and branding and advertising decisions. Franchise owners in the 1950s received a detailed *McDonald's Manual* that ran seventy-five pages and covered topics including "food specifications," "store opening procedure," "job turnover," and "cleaning and maintenance"—of the walk-in refrigerator, the potato peeler, the syrup pumps, and much else. It also listed retail prices:

Hamburgers	15 cents
Cheeseburgers	19 cents
Triple thick milkshakes	20 cents
French fries	10 cents
Root Beer, Coca-Cola, and Orange	10 cents or 15 cents
Half pint milk	10 cents
Coffee	10 cents
Hot chocolate (in winter)	12 cents
Old fashion pound cake	15 cents

By 1963, there were more than 300 McDonald's restaurants across thirty-seven states.

International business

After 1945, American investment and funds came to play an essential role in the rebuilding of Europe as part of the Marshall Plan, named for Secretary of State George Marshall. Under the Marshall Plan, the United States gave more than $13 billion (about $110 billion in 2020 dollars) from 1948 to 1952 to rebuild western Europe and restore political stability. The plan aimed to modernize European industry, improve prosperity, increase access to coal and other needed resources, and combat the spread of Communism. Roughly one-third ($4.4 billion) of the money went to Great Britain and just under one-sixth ($1.9 billion) to France. West Germany received roughly one-tenth because the restoration of Germany was thought essential to support prosperity in other European countries that depended on German resources and manufactured goods, thereby preventing the spread of Soviet influence.

Along with the Marshall Plan, US companies increased their global footprint. Major US oil companies, including Jersey Standard, rebuilt damaged refineries and expanded their presence across western Europe, seeking to take advantage of the need for petroleum products during the recovery period.

The 1960s also saw the increase of US foreign investments in manufacturing and wholesale and retail trading. Prominent industries investing abroad included transportation equipment, chemicals, machinery, food products, electrical machinery, and primary and fabricated metals. In wholesale and retail, Sears, Roebuck—the largest American merchandiser—began expanding its business into Latin America and Europe. The supermarket chain Safeway (founded in 1915) started to invest in Europe and Australia. By 1966, it had 28 stores in Britain, 5 in Germany, 11 in Australia, and 241 in Canada.

Accompanying US business abroad was the expansion of advertising, accounting, market research, and management consultant firms. The consulting firm McKinsey & Company grew in the 1940s and 1950s and promoted the M-Form and other US management strategies in Europe. By the end of the 1960s, McKinsey's European clients included Cadbury, Cunard, and Rolls-Royce in the United Kingdom; Nestlé, Geigy, and Sandoz in

Switzerland; KLM and Royal Dutch Shell in the Netherlands; and Volkswagen, Deutsche Bank, and BASF in Germany.

As American companies increased their business overseas, so international companies began to enter American markets. The American auto industry, for example, was challenged by Germany's Volkswagen (which formed Volkswagen of America in 1955) and Japan's Toyota—both of which made successful entries into the US automobile market in the 1950s and 1960s. Both offered smaller cars, an unfilled niche in the American car market. The Volkswagen Beetle, with its replaceable parts and simple design, proved especially popular in the early 1960s against the "chrome cathedrals" produced in Detroit, but it, too, faced competition. In 1958, Toyota began marketing its Crown automobile in the United States, but it was underpowered and flopped. In 1968, the company's more powerful Corolla did much better, and by 1975, the Japanese car manufacturer replaced Volkswagen as the best-selling import brand in the country.

In response, American carmakers tried to move into the smaller-car market with offerings like the Chevrolet Corvair and Ford Falcon, both introduced in the 1960s. The Falcon was produced from 1960 to 1970 and exported to Argentina, Australia, Canada, Chile, and Mexico. The Corvair was initially very popular, but drivers were dissatisfied with its handling. In 1965, consumer activist Ralph Nader attacked the Corvair (and many other American car models) in his book *Unsafe at Any Speed*. Toyota outdid American competition through its famed "production system," which took decentralization beyond what Sloan had imagined. Toyota's approach revolved around a persistent effort to streamline systems to eliminate waste and allow flexible production for just-in-time delivery. By 1980, Japan surpassed the United States as the world's leading producer of automobiles.

In the final decades of the twentieth century, Japanese imports also gradually came to replace American products in other industries—for example, in televisions and other consumer electronics products. In 1955, US television manufacturers controlled 96 percent of the American market. A decade later, they held just 30 percent, with inexpensive Japanese imports gaining a strong foothold. By 1980, there were only three American television manufacturers left in the United States— RCA, Zenith, and GTE.

In response to rising global competition, many American firms pursued a new strategy that they hoped would allow them to regain a competitive advantage. They became conglomerates, bringing varied businesses in different industries together into a single group. The 1960s was dubbed "the age of the conglomerate," with more than 6,000 mergers and acquisitions in 1969 alone. Despite the rush to merge, however, the strategy was seldom successful.

One (albeit unsuccessful) advocate of the conglomerate strategy was RCA. The company had once been an enormous success; it had dominated the American market for radios and consumer electronics in the 1920s and 1930s and then moved into television starting in the 1940s. In the 1960s, however, it made a fateful move into computers, an area outside its core business, seeking to compete with IBM. It then made several unrelated acquisitions including Hertz Rent-a-Car, Random House publishing, and businesses in frozen food, carpets, and paper manufacturing, transforming itself from an electronics company into a highly diversified conglomerate. In 1986, this rapid and unrelated diversification ultimately brought an end to RCA. In its core market of consumer electronics rose four Japanese companies— Sony, Matsushita, Sanyo, and Sharp. Sony, especially, came to dominate digital technology. With Philips (a Dutch multinational), Sony introduced the compact disc in 1982 and the CD-ROM in 1985.

But it was not just overseas competition from Japan that threatened American business. During this period of uncertainty and turbulence in US markets, the country also experienced a destabilizing oil crisis. The United States had long been an oil-exporting nation. In 1920, for example, it produced 65 percent of the global oil supply, and even in the aftermath of World War II, it maintained a positive net export balance of 61,000 barrels per day.

However, beginning in the 1950s, in part because of the rapid growth of the automobile industry, domestic demand for oil began to outpace domestic production, and the United States became increasingly reliant on oil imports. Indeed, in 1950, the United States imported 850,000 barrels of oil per day. By 1960, that figure had risen to 1.8 million. This put the United States in a precarious situation as the balance of power among global oil producers began to shift. In 1960, major Middle Eastern oil-producing nations (Iran, Iraq, Kuwait, and Saudi Arabia) joined with Venezuela to form the Organization of the Petroleum Exporting Countries (OPEC), seeking to coordinate production and export policies among member nations to ensure steady returns to oil producers.

By 1970, US oil imports had risen to 3.4 million barrels per day, and global demand was also on the rise, straining the capacity of OPEC nations, which were already producing at 80 percent capacity. The first "oil shock" came in 1973. OPEC implemented an embargo against the United States and other nations that had supported Israel during the Yom Kippur War, resulting in a massive price spike as supply dropped. In 1979, a further drop in oil supply resulting from the Iranian Revolution, combined with steadily rising global demand, resulted in a second oil crisis. By 1980, the price of oil was twelve times what it had been in 1970.

During the 1970s, the United States experienced five quarters of decreasing gross domestic product, and the unemployment rate hit 9 percent in 1975. American companies needed very different strategies to fend off global competitors at home and to try to regain lost shares of global markets. Some economists, including Robert Heilbroner, became pessimistic about US business. In *Business Civilization in Decline* (1976), he argued that global capitalism had become too volatile to endure: "Much as we now inspect Chichen Itza, the Great Wall, the pyramids, Machu Picchu, so we may some day visit and marvel at the ruins of the great steel works at Sparrows Point, the atomic complex at Hanford, the computer centers at Houston." It was a far different business environment than just a few decades before.

Chapter 9
Entrepreneurs and the global economy, 1980–2020

In the decades from 1980 to the end of the twentieth century, the American business landscape changed markedly. The post-World War II period was the high point of *managerial capitalism,* during which managers at large US firms found markets for their products around the world. Executives and managers working at these firms often exhibited a strong degree of loyalty to their enterprises, banks were heavily regulated and pursued strategies of low risk and steady profits, and union membership was relatively high (about 35 percent of private-sector workers were union members in the mid-1950s).

By contrast, the closing decades of the twentieth century were more difficult to categorize, with several important yet disparate developments that significantly affected American business. First, these decades were marked by deregulation. Starting in the late 1970s, American policymakers sought to reduce government restrictions in some industries to try to make companies more competitive. President Jimmy Carter signed the Airline Deregulation Act of 1978, the Motor Carrier Act of 1980, which deregulated trucking, and the Staggers Rail Act of 1980, which deregulated the railroad industry—an industry that, over decades, had suffered dramatically from automobile and trucking competition. His successor, Ronald Reagan, extended deregulation to include interstate bussing, ocean shipping, and other industries.

This wave of deregulation was in concert with the work of Nobel laureate Milton Friedman, who promoted the idea of free-market economics to combat rising unemployment and inflation. The application of such ideas, especially during the Reagan presidency, represented a major departure from the thinking of the New Deal. Reagan proclaimed in his inaugural address, "Government is not the solution to our problem, government is the problem."

Second, the closing decades of the twentieth century saw the rise of *shareholder capitalism*, a term popularized by Friedman, in which the long-standing balance of power among shareholders, boards of directors, and managers began to shift. Previously, shareholders at large public companies could seldom influence managers or executives. However, beginning in the 1970s, institutional investors, such as giant pension funds and hedge funds, began to grow large enough to monitor and even influence corporate leaders. Board members and shareholders became increasingly active in response to increased international competition, corporate failures (such as the massive Penn Central bankruptcy in 1970), and strategic mistakes (including the wave of conglomerates and divestitures). Moreover, in the 1980s, reports of "hostile takeovers" and "corporate raiders" became increasingly common, as shareholders found other, more aggressive, ways to circumvent the authority of corporate managers.

In response to these developments, businesses started to rethink their understanding of *corporate governance*—who runs a corporation and how it is structured—as the power of managers and executives waned in comparison to that of increasingly powerful directors and shareholders. Notions about how to measure a company's valuation began to change in parallel. While previously tied to corporate assets, products, employees, and other concrete metrics, in the 1970s valuation shifted toward a market-driven approach. The economist Michael Jensen argued that companies should focus on "shareholder return" and advocated for tying the compensation of CEOs to stock market performance—an idea that contributed to skyrocketing payment packages.

Finally, the closing decades of the twentieth century were also a period of financial innovation, as banks broke away from the relatively conservative strategies of the 1950s and 1960s. This shift was largely the result of a more lenient regulatory environment—evidenced, especially, by the 1999 repeal of the Depression-era Glass–Steagall Act, which had mandated the separation of commercial and investment banks. In the same years, activity on the stock market grew rapidly. While roughly 160 million shares were traded per day on the New York Stock Exchange in 1990, that figure rose to 1.6 billion in the early twenty-first century. The financial future of many Americans became entwined in the activities of the market, as nearly one-quarter of household wealth was tied to stocks. Financial transactions also became more complex as hedge funds, which pooled money from institutional investors, increased in numbers and operated in "derivatives," new higher-risk products derived from conventional securities.

In the context of this changing business landscape, computer technologies proliferated in the final decades of the twentieth century with important impacts on oversight, governance, and finance by improving communication, calculation, and information processing.

Silicon Valley

While many large-scale companies in traditional sectors—for example, automobiles and consumer electronics—were rethinking their strategy and structure, a new site of innovation emerged on the West Coast, stretching from San Jose to Seattle. It would become a center for high-tech industries such as computing, aviation, and advanced engineering.

The growth of a high-tech cluster on the West Coast would have seemed unlikely in the period immediately after World War II. Then, the nascent computer industry came to be dominated by established firms, including IBM and the so-called Seven Dwarfs—NCR (founded in Dayton, OH), Sperry Rand (Brooklyn, NY), Control Data (Minneapolis, MN), General Electric (Schenectady, NY), RCA (New York, NY), Honeywell (Wabash, IN), and Burroughs (Plymouth, MI)—which were all located east of, or near, the Mississippi River. Moreover, with Digital Equipment Corporation and Wang, the area around Boston's Route 128 led the development of the minicomputer, a smaller and more affordable alternative to mainframes.

After the 1970s, however, the center of technological innovation in computers shifted to the West Coast. The small strip of California known now as Silicon Valley began as a fertile stretch of land filled with plum, almond, and apricot orchards. The area's fruit-drying and -packing plants had been transformed to perform war production during World War II, and after the war, Lockheed, Northrup Grumman, and Litton Industries used the facilities to produce aircraft, radios, and engines for the civilian economy. Beginning in the 1960s, the area started to establish itself as a center for innovation in the sciences and, importantly, in technology.

Frederick Terman, a professor of engineering at Stanford University, was a pioneering figure in the early years of Silicon Valley. In 1945, Terman became dean of the engineering school and, a decade later, university provost. He believed that universities were a "natural resource" for industry—a necessary element of technological entrepreneurship. As Terman wrote, "Industry is finding that, for activities involving a high level of scientific and technological creativity, a location in a center of brains is more important than a location near markets, raw materials, transportation, or factory labor." In this spirit, Terman set aside 209 acres of university land in 1951 to lease to private tech companies. Stanford Industrial Park, as it was known, became home to Hewlett–Packard, Lockheed, Xerox (PARC), Varian Associates, and GE, among others. Terman fostered academy–industry cooperation by encouraging faculty consulting, inviting industrial researchers to teach specialized courses, and creating an honors cooperative program that allowed students to earn degrees while working full-time.

Fairchild and Intel

One of the most influential figures in Silicon Valley was William Shockley. A solid-state physicist trained at the Massachusetts Institute of Technology, Shockley was instrumental in the invention and development of the transistor in the 1940s. In 1954 he left Bell Labs in New Jersey and moved to Palo Alto, where he had spent his youth. There, he started a transistor manufacturing company called Shockley Semiconductor Laboratory. He was among the first to use silicon to build transistors, rather than the more commonly used germanium.

Despite Shockley's early success, his autocratic management style and erratic personality prompted mutiny when he decided to stop research into silicon-based semiconductors. Eight senior scientists left Shockley Semiconductor and, with a $1 million investment from New York financiers Arthur Rock and Sherman Fairchild, established Fairchild Semiconductors in 1957. Two of the so-called Traitorous Eight—Robert Noyce and Gordon Moore—soon left Fairchild Semiconductor in 1968 to found Intel, where they continued work on memory chips and eventually the microprocessors that revolutionized computing technology.

In 1965, Moore made a prediction, known to posterity as "Moore's Law." He estimated that the number of transistors on a single microchip would double every year. (In 1975, he revised the estimate to every two years.) He was right: Computing capacity doubled at the pace he predicted until the end of the twentieth century. In 1960, a single transistor cost about a dollar. At the end of the century, a single dollar could buy 10 million transistors. As the devices got smaller, they also got more powerful and more efficient. By 1976, Intel was the largest supplier of semiconductor components in the world. By 1979, profits there reached $78 million—nearly forty times what the company had earned in 1972.

Like Intel, many tech start-ups received support from venture capital funds. In 1961, New York–based Arthur Rock moved to California and, in partnership with Thomas A. Davis Jr., founded the venture capital firm Davis & Rock, which, in addition to Fairchild and Intel, invested in Apple, Scientific Data Systems, and Teledyne. The collaboration between scientists, entrepreneurs, educators, federal and state research sponsors, and venture capitalists allowed Silicon Valley to blossom into a center of innovation, with the natural boundaries of mountain and ocean keeping companies in collaborative proximity. By the 1990s, the region was the fastest-growing high-tech sector in the country—with more than 250,000 employees working in high-tech jobs.

Silicon Valley firms also became notable for their distinct corporate culture. Employees did not expect career-long employment as they had in big firms in the 1950s and 1960s. Instead, the phenomenon of *job-hopping*—staying less than two years in a particular company—became increasingly common. Day-to-day work culture was less formal, with more casual dress; corporate architecture was flatter; and the upper levels of management were slightly more diverse. Although they were by no means representative of the diversity of American society, firms were nonetheless more inclusive than the homogenous ranks of managers described in Whyte's *Organization Man* (1956). Silicon Valley firms came to draw talent from all over the world; in 1998, entrepreneurs originally from China and India were running 25 percent of start-ups in the region.

The rapid rise of Silicon Valley led to renewed interest in understanding the cycles of corporate growth and failure in the

10. In this declassified CIA satellite image of University Avenue in Palo Alto, California, in 1984, buildings and streets resemble silicon chips, transistors, and resistors in a circuit board. In the technology behind the map and the details of the image, it depicts a world shaped by enterprise, far removed from that of colonial cartographers featured earlier in this book.

1990s. In *Innovator's Dilemma* (1997), Harvard Business School professor Clayton Christensen looked to the work of Joseph Schumpeter, an Austrian-born political economist. Schumpeter coined the phrase "creative destruction" to describe the process through which entrepreneurs continually disrupted existing firms and work traditions by making innovations in technology, management, marketing, or finance. Christensen applied this idea to explain why well-managed, leading companies had fallen behind. He noted the demise of Sears in the face of discount retailers, IBM in the area of minicomputers, and Xerox in the era of personal computers and desktop copiers. Technological innovation, Christensen argued, demanded a different type of management than that which had built and sustained successful companies in the past. Because large companies focused on incremental improvements to products for their established customers, they tended not to invest in emerging technology markets. Smaller, nimbler, more "entrepreneurial" firms, by contrast, were not hindered by bureaucracy and could target new customer bases and "disrupt" the market with the introduction of new products, patented technology, and services.

The personal computer

Perhaps the most disruptive new technology of the late twentieth century was the personal computer. In the early 1970s, Intel, Texas Instruments, Motorola, and others were producing integrated circuits, mostly to provide memory for large mainframe computers. There was also a growing number of hobbyists and tinkerers eager to experiment with new technology. The Homebrew Computer Club, founded in 1975 in Menlo Park, provided a place for enthusiasts to gather, share new ideas, and view new inventions. Steve Wozniak, who attended Berkeley and had an immense talent for engineering design, went to one such club meeting and afterward set out to build what would become the Apple I computer.

Apple cofounder Steve Jobs was instrumental to the early success of the company. Rather than just selling the design to an established firm, Jobs convinced Wozniak that they could make and market the computer themselves, and they set up a makeshift manufacturing operation in Jobs's garage. In 1976, the Apple I, which was a well-thought-out circuit board that could be attached to a screen or monitor, was launched. They sold the Apple I in an electronics store called the Byte Shop for $500 each. The Apple II—which featured an integrated screen and keyboard and a floppy disc drive for additional data storage—was released the following year and was more marketable. In less than ten years, Apple had sold more than 2 million Apple II computers.

The main difference between Wozniak's design and existing prototypes for nonindustrial computers was its focus on the potential needs of the home user. Its graphic display, which Wozniak had built with an old television, was more advanced and visually appealing than anything else on the market. This focus on the user's experience and the possibilities of nonbusiness use for the computer turned out to be the keys to Apple's survival in the face of competition.

Indeed, Apple did not have the market to itself for long. IBM, which had been the largest company in the mainframe computing market, soon established an independent unit devoted to the development of a desktop computer, or personal computer (PC). To bring a product quickly to market, executives decided to outsource the production of the microprocessor, memory, and software. Microsoft, founded in 1975 by Bill Gates and Paul Allen, won the contract to develop the computer's operating system.

In 1981, the IBM Personal Computer was officially introduced, with a price tag of $1,565, and it was wildly successful. Sales were so great that in 1983 the company created a division to manage the manufacturing and distribution of the PC. This group's output and revenues were large enough that, had it been an independent company, it would have made the Fortune 500 list that year. In 1985, Microsoft introduced a new operating system, Windows 1.0, an advance that introduced a point-and-click interface.

IBM's decision not to build its own software or a proprietary operating system led to a boom in entrepreneurial firms creating peripheral components and software applications for the IBM PC. Rather than competing by making new operating platforms, innovators focused on designing software for spreadsheets, management databases, word processing, graphic design, and finance. However, although sharing its operating system had allowed IBM's PC to become the industry standard, it also enabled competitors to build clones. Eventually, some of the firms that used its operating system began to mass-produce high-quality imitators of the PC. Companies including Compaq, Dell, and Gateway steadily attracted IBM customers.

Apple avoided this problem in large part thanks to Steve Jobs's belief that the company needed to control both hardware and software design to achieve a seamless user experience—a strategy he met with the release of the Macintosh computer in 1984 and later with the iPod (2001), iPhone (2007), and iPad (2010). Apple even introduced its own iTunes store in 2001, an online platform that allowed users to purchase and sync music to their Apple devices. Jobs's insistence on integrating aesthetics and function, as well as his emphasis on graphic interface and user-friendliness, helped build customer loyalty. In this respect, Jobs was inspired by Polaroid founder Edwin Land, who believed that a successful business must incorporate elements of both science and art. However, Jobs's appeal went far beyond customer loyalty. His mark on the company was so strong that soon people referred to "the cult of Steve Jobs." His rise from humble beginnings, and his production of truly beautiful technology, endeared him to many around the world. In 2018, Apple became the first American trillion-dollar corporation, just over a century after U.S. Steel became the nation's first billion-dollar corporation (in 1901).

In the 1980s the rest of American business looked to Silicon Valley and aimed to harness the entrepreneurial spirit that flourished in the Bay Area. The admiration for Jobs extended to the American business community and rekindled respect for entrepreneurial values and charismatic CEOs. Such thinking helped to set the scene for business leaders such as Lee Iacocca, who sought to revive the struggling Chrysler Motor Company in the 1980s, bringing out the Dodge Caravan and Plymouth Voyager and promoting smaller cars, like the Dodge Omni and Plymouth Horizon.

The Internet

"The Internet did not originate in the business world," wrote sociologist Manuel Castells; "It was too daring a technology, too expensive a project, and too risky an initiative to be assumed by profit-oriented organizations." Instead, the communication technology now called the Internet was pioneered by the Department of Defense, specifically the Information Processing Techniques Office of the Advanced Research Projects Agency. After the launch of the Soviet satellite *Sputnik* in 1957, the United States redoubled efforts to outpace the Soviet Union with superior military technology. ARPANET, the first network enabling interactive computing, was one innovation to come out of this military research agenda. Initially limited to use in government and academic research, by the mid-1990s this network technology was opened up for public and commercial use—marking the advent of the World Wide Web, invented by the English computer scientist Tim Berners-Lee, which revolutionized the way business was done around the globe.

To make the Web viable, Netscape Communications developed the Netscape Navigator browser in 1994, and Microsoft released Internet Explorer the following year. By 1994, there were about 2,700 websites, including ones for the White House, the *Economist* magazine, and a fan site for the animated television show *The Simpsons*. (Roughly twenty-five years later, there were an estimated 1 billion websites.) With the personal computer and the Internet, businesses suddenly had the capacity for the constant and almost instantaneous exchange of information.

The Internet diffused rapidly. By 2014, about 75 percent of Americans owned either a desktop or a portable laptop computer that could access the Internet. Globally, about 38 percent of the world's population owned a computer. In the 2010s, with the rise of the smartphone and the spectacular range of applications made for it, this figure increased dramatically. In 2011, just 35 percent of Americans owned a smartphone. By 2018, that number had grown to nearly 80 percent. In less than forty years, individually owned computers had gone from being isolated devices, the size of televisions, to fitting into a coat pocket, instantly available, and connected to machines around the world.

Personal computers, the Internet, and smartphones changed the strategies of business in nearly every industry—including manufacturing, services, transportation, and retail (for instance, with inventory-tracking and point-of-sale registers). Computers also brought transformational change to the financial services industry. In 1950, banks did not have computers. By the early twenty-first century, every facet of the banking industry depended on them, from interaction with users (through ATMs and online banking portals) to internal management, research, tracking investments, handling foreign currency, and competition with other banks.

Crisis and aftermath

Regulators and investors had difficulty monitoring and evaluating the new Internet-based business ventures. The dot-com bubble of 1995 to 2000, for example, was a period of excessive speculation in Internet stocks, with some new initial public offerings achieving lasting success, but many more failing. (The Internet apparel company Boo.com, for instance, raised $185 million in venture capital funds, but the company lasted only about eighteen months.)

As a result, the early 2000s experienced a period of both financial innovation and financial scandal. Perhaps the best-known example was the energy company Enron, which eventually folded after revelations in 2001 of long-term fraud and corruption. The extent of the fraud was such that Enron's failure had reverberating impacts across much of the financial services industry and led to the passage of the Sarbanes–Oxley Act (2002), which required greater transparency in the filing of financial reports.

The great crisis, however, was yet to come. The global financial crisis of 2007–8 began in the subprime mortgage markets and then escalated into a global banking crisis. One casualty was New York–based Lehman Brothers, the international financial services firm founded in 1844 as a dry goods business in Alabama. In the early 2000s, Lehman Brothers, then under the direction of CEO Richard Fuld, became a leader in the subprime mortgage industry—mortgages granted to individuals with poor credit scores. Banks compensated for the high risk associated with these mortgages by charging borrowers higher interest rates. In 2006 alone, Lehman securitized $146 billion in subprime mortgages. But that year also saw rising rates of loan default and home foreclosures. Lehman, which purported to have made tens of billions of dollars in home loans, declared bankruptcy in 2008. Washington Mutual Bank, then the United States' largest savings and loan association, also went bankrupt.

In 2008, the federal government bailed out another failing group, the American International Group, for $180 billion, in part because of the idea that it was "too big to fail"—meaning that its collapse would also bring down its trading partners, including Goldman Sachs, Morgan Stanley, and Bank of America. The widespread financial crisis was followed by a global downturn called the Great Recession, which lasted through 2010.

The Great Recession marked a period of transition for Silicon Valley and Seattle. The West Coast, known as being a hub for entrepreneurial start-ups, became the home of several massive corporations that had weathered the crisis, including some that had been around for decades, such as Apple and Microsoft, and some new ones, such as the e-retailer Amazon (founded in 1994), the search engine Google (1998), and the social media company Facebook (2004).

These multinational companies came to dominate many product areas beyond their original interests. Google launched a number of programs that offered users astonishing amounts of information and new capabilities, including Google Earth (2001), Google Maps (2005), and Google Translate (2006). Google also became a provider of content with the $1.65 billion acquisition of YouTube in 2006 and a manufacturer of hardware with the introduction of its own smartphone in 2010.

Amazon was another impressive example of large-scale global diversification. Jeff Bezos got the idea for his Web-based "everything store" while working at a New York hedge fund in the 1990s. At first dubious about commercial applications of the Web, Bezos was impressed by the record-breaking growth of Internet usage in the early 1990s. He became convinced that the Internet was the next major retail platform, both because of its broad accessibility and because, freed from the limitations of traditional stores, it allowed companies to offer consumers comparatively limitless selection.

Amazon began as an Internet retailer selling nothing but books. After just one year in operation it had 180,000 customer accounts and took in $16 million in revenue. It proved enormously disruptive to the publishing industry and, by 1998, its sales exceeded that of Barnes & Noble and Borders, then the largest brick-and-mortar booksellers. It then began to sell music and videos and then toys, software, games, and consumer electronics, on its way to becoming the largest Internet retailer in the world, by revenue, and a leading multinational in e-commerce, cloud computing, and digital streaming. The legal scholar Lina Khan compared Bezos's strategy to John D. Rockefeller's at Standard Oil in the late nineteenth century: like Rockefeller, Bezos worked deliberately to build a business that could not only capture market share rapidly, but also defend against new market entrants, for example, by engaging in predatory pricing.

Another part of Amazon's strength lay in its leveraging of user data. Through analyzing clicks on its website, Amazon gleaned detailed, in-depth information—never before available to retailers or businesses of any kind—on the millions of users who freely shared their likes, product preferences, and consumption habits. The acquisition of user data by the largest Internet companies, including Amazon, Facebook, and Google, marked the emergence of a new business model, as companies turned human experience—including everything from personal photos, correspondence, exercise metrics, shopping preferences, and much more—into data to be bought and sold. Moreover, this information was analyzed, shared, and fed into mathematical formulas that sought to predict individual behavior and to modify what news, advertisements, and prices consumers would see. For many, the harvesting and application of such data had chilling consequences for the rights to personal information.

The computer industry had undergone a remarkable transformation in the years since the personal computer was introduced. By 2020, on the Fortune 500 list, Amazon, Apple, Google (Alphabet), Facebook, and Microsoft were well above oil companies (including Exxon Mobil), automobile companies (such as GM) and traditional strong performers (including Coca-Cola and GE) in terms of market value. Moreover, the activities of these new Internet-based firms were so vast as to raise deep political and social questions—just as, for instance, automobile companies had in the twentieth century in terms of pollution and personal safety. For most users of new Internet services, the problem was how to balance the benefits of seemingly limitless information with concerns about privacy. For the business scholar Shoshana Zuboff, the problem was more far-reaching. She argued that such web-based firms had introduced a new and dangerous form of "surveillance capitalism," one that was still only in its infancy and one that would pose a continuing challenge for regulators and the public.

Conclusion: Sustainability

For much of its history, the United States has been, to admirers and critics alike, a bellwether for democratic capitalism around the world. The rise of American business has not been linear, but turbulent and episodic, marked by bursts of innovation by new firms, with new technologies, products, and services. Several key innovative industries, centered in different cities, sparked economic development, including, for instance, textiles in Lowell, steel in Pittsburgh, meatpacking in Chicago, automobiles in Detroit, and personal computers in San Francisco, to name a few. Entrepreneurs also introduced seminal institutional innovations, including the factory, corporation, the modern financial system, and the Internet-based firm. These innovations, often fought by established interests, brought tumult to existing methods of business and frequently unleashed the destructive features of capitalism, including shuttered factories, unemployed workers, and failed companies. This cycle of creative innovation and disruption has been a long-standing feature of US economic growth. The economist Joseph Schumpeter noted, "Constant, relentless change is the hallmark of capitalism."

The place that business came to occupy in American society was neither organic nor accidental but has been shaped by policymaking and by America's democratic culture. A central tension in the history of American business has been the effort by policymakers to enable entrepreneurial energy and encourage innovation, on the one hand, and to mitigate against the most destructive elements of capitalism, on the other. Hence, policymaking in the United States has emphasized, in general, infrequent, yet targeted, involvement in economic affairs. In the nineteenth century, government policy encouraged entrepreneurs to take risks in order to promote the development of American industry. Major legislation from this period included limited liability, bankruptcy protection, general incorporation laws, land grants to railroads, and other subsidies to business enterprises. In the twentieth century, progressive reform sought to improve worker rights and welfare in the industrial economy and to provide social security for American citizens.

Business in America has prospered also due to a culture of entrepreneurship. Especially in the decades since World War II policymakers, pressured by social movements and legal challenges, undertook efforts to make business opportunity more inclusive. A belief in the ability to prosper through business has been present almost from the founding of the country, and though often denied to many Americans based on race, gender, and ethnicity, has nonetheless endured as a core value. Indeed, the aspiration to pursue economic opportunities has inspired immigrants from around the world to come to the United States. This democratic aspect of the US economy is often cited as an explanation for why American society is especially tolerant of the turbulent and chaotic nature of capitalism. As the *Economist* noted in the mid-1990s, "Whereas in Germany and Japan a businessman who fails suffers a permanent stigma, Americans smile benignly on entrepreneurs who go bust, and this gives the society as a whole an invaluable license to experiment."

More recently, however, American business has been the subject of frequent criticism. Over the past decade, the pace of innovation—in information technology, investing, overseas manufacturing, social media platforms, and app-based businesses—has been so rapid that it has challenged effective regulation. At the same time, changing trends in international politics and a retreat from globalization have compounded economic uncertainty. A range of observers have questioned whether business in the United States is becoming less democratic and, indeed, whether American-style capitalism is sustainable.

One criticism has focused on the idea that business has contributed to growing inequities in wealth, with profits increasingly going to corporate leaders and to the country's wealthiest "1 percent." Such concerns came to the fore during the "Occupy Wall Street" movement, in which protestors occupied a park in lower Manhattan for two months in the fall of 2011. Among other things, the group protested the influence of corporations on politics, as exemplified by the controversial Supreme Court case, *Citizens United v. Federal Election Commission* (2010), which overturned prior restrictions on corporate spending on political campaigns.

Shortly after, French economist Thomas Piketty published what would become a key text of the period, *Capital in the Twenty-First Century* (2013), which brought together, in crushing detail, a history of rising wealth inequality in the United States and Europe. Though a dense, scholarly work, the book became a bestseller, arguing that unless countries worked to intervene, capitalism would erode democratic societies through escalating disparities in wealth.

In addition to concerns about rising income inequality, other critics have pointed out the massive environmental damage caused by the burning of fossil fuels. Large corporations in the transportation, energy, and manufacturing sectors have all contributed to global warming, which brought flooding in coastal regions (and hence threatened many of the world's largest cities), extreme and unpredictable weather patterns, and agricultural destruction, especially as a result of drought and fire. In response to this criticism, some companies sought to become more "green."

Walmart, for instance, invested in using some forms of renewable energy in its stores. At the same time, the electric car industry, led in the United States by Tesla, offered an alternative to petroleum-based cars. But the scale of global climate change was overwhelming. In 2016, renewable energy sources, including geothermal and solar heat and wind energy, accounted for less than 20 percent of the world's energy needs.

Amid these concerns, some writers have described the first decades of the 2000s as a "New Gilded Age," recalling the period in the late nineteenth century when wealthy business titans held immense political and social power, while industrial workers toiled long hours in often brutal conditions. That earlier period was also one of powerful critiques and penetrating analyses of American business, which prompted a period of regulatory reform during the Progressive Era that shaped the modern corporation.

If the past is any guide, the New Gilded Age may motivate a similar period of public outcry and of legislative reform to address the problems of the twenty-first century. In *Reimagining Capitalism* (2020), economist Rebecca Henderson was among those who argued that business leaders themselves must play a leading role in changing ideas about the nature of business—and thus work to gain public trust and confidence as stewards of economic, political, and social power.

Whether the United States will continue to be the exemplar of democratic capitalism depends on whether it succeeds in addressing these fundamental issues with effective policymaking and regulation and also whether it maintains an environment that encourages entrepreneurship and innovation. As this history has shown, the American economy has grown, in large part, because entrepreneurs from around the world have sought to pursue their commercial ambitions, to invest their capital, and to develop their ideas in the United States. Whether they will continue to do so in the future is uncertain.

References

Introduction: A business civilization

James Truslow Adams, *Our Business Civilization: Some Aspects of American Culture* (New York: A. C. Boni, 1929), 16.

Sven Beckert, "History of American Capitalism," in *American History Now*, ed. Eric Foner and Lisa McGirr (Philadelphia: Temple University Press, 2011), 314.

Chapter 1

James Truslow Adams, *The Epic of America* (Boston: Little, Brown, 1931), xx.

Chapter 2

Charles Dickens, *American Notes* (1842; repr., Carlisle, MA: Applewood Books, 1850), 169.

Chapter 3

Proprietors of the Charles River Bridge v. Proprietors of the Warren Bridge, 36 U.S. 420, 423 (1837).

Speech of Mr. Appleton, of Massachusetts, Delivered in the House of Representatives of the U.S., 30 May 1832 (Washington, DC: Gales and Seaton, 1832), 17.

Charles Dickens, *American Notes* (1842; repr., Carlisle, MA: Applewood Books, 1850), 46.

From Thomas Jefferson to John Jay, 30 August 1785, Founders Online, National Archives, accessed September 29, 2019, https://founders.archives.gov/documents/Jefferson/01-08-02-0354.

Thomas Chandler Haliburton, *The Clockmaker; or The Sayings and Doings of Sam Slick* (1836; repr., London: Richard Bentley, 1843), 9.

Joseph Whitworth and George Wallis, *The American System of Manufactures: The Report of the Committee on the Machinery of the United States* (Edinburgh: Edinburgh University Press, 1855), 281.

Chapter 4

Daniel McCallum quoted in Alfred Chandler, *The Railroads: The Nation's First Big Business* (New York: Arno Press, 1981), 102–5. Originally printed in Daniel McCallum, "Superintendent's Report," *Erie Annual Report* (1855).

The McCormick Harvesting Machine Company, *The Century of the Reaper* (New York: Houghton Mifflin, 1931), 98.

Chapter 5

Thomas Mellon, *Thomas Mellon and His Times: Printed for His Family and Descendants Exclusively* (1885; repr., Pittsburgh: University of Pittsburgh Press, 1994), 33.

Ida M. Tarbell, *The History of the Standard Oil Company*, two volumes in one (1904; repr., Gloucester, MA: Peter Smith, 1963), 2:287.

Chapter 6

Henry Ford with Samuel Crowther, *Moving Forward* (Garden City, NY: Doubleday, 1931), 28–29.

Frederick Winslow Taylor, *The Principles of Scientific Management* (Norwood, MA: Plimpton Press, 1911), 47.

"Gives $10,000,000 to 26,000 Employees," *New York Times*, January 6, 1914, 1.

Peter Drucker, *Management: Tasks, Responsibilities, Practices* (1974; rev. ed., New York: HarperCollins, 2008), 14.

Alfred P. Sloan, *My Years with General Motors* (1963; repr., New York: Doubleday, 1990), 265.

Richard Tedlow, *New and Improved: The Story of Mass Marketing in America* (1990; repr., Boston: Harvard Business School Press, 1996), 8.

Chapter 7

Herbert Hoover, *The New Day: Campaign Speeches of Herbert Hoover, 1928* (Stanford, CA: Stanford University Press, 1928), 16.

Raymond Moley, *After Seven Years* (London: Harper & Bros., 1939), 155.

Thomas J. Watson, *Father Son & Co.: My Life at IBM and Beyond* (New York: Bantam Books, 1990), 33.

Donald Nelson, *Arsenal of Democracy: The Story of American War Production* (1946; repr., New York: Da Capo Press, 1973), 76, 212–13, 237.

Alfred P. Sloan, *My Years with General Motors* (1963; repr., New York: Doubleday, 1990), 377.

Richard Rhodes, *The Making of the Atomic Bomb* (New York: Simon & Schuster, 1986), 500.

Chapter 8

Alfred D. Chandler, "The Competitive Performance of U.S. Industrial Enterprises since the Second World War," *Business History Review* 68, no. 1 (Spring 1994): 23–25.

Tom Watson, *Father, Son & Co.* (New York: Bantam Books, 1990), ix.

Robert L. Heilbroner, *Business Civilization in Decline* (New York: W. W. Norton, 1976), 122–23.

Chapter 9

Ronald Reagan, *Speaking My Mind: Selected Speeches* (New York: Simon & Schuster), 61.

Frederick Terman quoted in Stuart W. Leslie and Robert H. Kargon, "Selling Silicon Valley: Frederick Terman's Model for Regional Advantage," *Business History Review* 70, no. 4 (Winter 1996): 437.

Manuel Castells, *The Internet Galaxy: Reflections on the Internet, Business, and Society* (Oxford: Oxford University Press, 2001), 22.

Conclusion: Sustainability

Anonymous, *The Economist* 336, no. 7932 (September 1995): SS14.

Further reading

General

Blackford, Mansel. *A History of Small Business in America*. Chapel Hill: University of North Carolina Press, 2003.

Bruchey, Stuart Weems. *Enterprise: The Dynamic Economy of a Free People*. Cambridge, MA: Harvard University Press, 1990.

Chandler, Alfred D. *Scale and Scope: The Dynamics of Industrial Capitalism*. Cambridge, MA: Belknap Press, 1990.

Chandler, Alfred D. *The Visible Hand: The Managerial Revolution in American Business*. Cambridge, MA: Harvard University Press, 1977.

Cochran, Thomas C. *Business in American Life*. New York: McGraw–Hill, 1972.

Lamoreaux, Naomi R., and William J. Novak, eds. *Corporations and American Democracy*. Cambridge, MA: Harvard University Press, 2017.

McCraw, Thomas K., and William R. Childs. *American Business since 1920: How It Worked*. Wheeling, IL: Harlan Davidson, 2009.

Moss, David. *Democracy: A Case Study*. Cambridge, MA: Harvard University Press, 2017.

Scranton, Philip. *Endless Novelty: Specialty Production and American Industrialization, 1865–1925*. Princeton, NJ: Princeton University Press, 1997.

Waterhouse, Benjamin. *Land of Enterprise: A Business History of the United States*. New York: Simon & Schuster, 2017.

Trade and empire

Bailyn, Bernard. *The Peopling of British North America: An Introduction*. New York: Random House, 1986.

Bruchey, Stuart Weems. *Robert Oliver, Merchant of Baltimore*. Baltimore: Johns Hopkins University Press, 1955.

Cullen, Jim. *The American Dream: A Short History of an Idea That Shaped a Nation*. New York: Oxford University Press, 2003.

Doerflinger, Thomas M. *A Vigorous Spirit of Enterprise: Merchants and Economic Development in Revolutionary Philadelphia*. Chapel Hill: University of North Carolina Press, 1986.

Hofstadter, Richard. *America at 1750: A Social Portrait*. New York: Alfred A. Knopf, 1971.

Perkins, Edward J. *The Economy of Colonial America*. New York: Columbia University Press, 1988.

Reinert, Sophus A. "The Way to Wealth around the World: Benjamin Franklin and the Globalization of American Capitalism." *American Historical Review* 120, no. 1 (2015): 61–97.

Taylor, Alan. *American Colonies*. New York: Viking Books, 2001.

Commerce in the new nation

Baptist, Edward. *The Half Has Never Been Told: Slavery and the Making of American Capitalism*. New York: Basic Books, 2014.

Beckert, Sven. *Empire of Cotton: A Global History*. New York: Alfred A. Knopf, 2015.

Davis, Lance E., Robert E. Gallman, and Karin Gleiter. *In Pursuit of Leviathan*. Chicago: University of Chicago Press, 1997.

McCraw, Thomas K. *The Founders and Finance: How Hamilton, Gallatin, and Other Immigrants Forged a New Economy*. Cambridge, MA: Harvard University Press, 2012.

Nicholas, Tom. *VC: An American History*. Cambridge, MA: Harvard University Press, 2019.

Olegario, Rowena. *Engine of Enterprise: Credit in America*. Cambridge, MA: Harvard University Press, 2016.

Porter, Kenneth Wiggins. *John Jacob Astor: Volumes I and II*. Cambridge, MA: Harvard University Press, 1930.

Rosenthal, Caitlin. *Accounting for Slavery: Masters and Management*. Cambridge, MA: Harvard University Press, 2018.

Scarborough, William. *Masters of the Big House: Elite Slaveholders of the Mid-Nineteenth Century South*. Baton Rouge: Louisiana State University Press, 2003.

Sylla, Richard, and Robert Wright. *Genealogy of American Finance.* New York: Columbia Business School Publishing, 2015.

Wright, Robert E. *The Poverty of Slavery: How Unfree Labor Pollutes the Economy.* Cham, Switzerland: Palgrave Macmillan, 2017.

Early manufacturers

Friedman, Walter A. *Birth of a Salesman: The Transformation of Selling in America.* Cambridge, MA: Harvard University Press, 2004.

Gibb, George Sweet. *The Saco-Lowell Shops: Textile Machinery Building in New England.* Cambridge, MA: Harvard University Press, 1950.

Harris, Neil. *Humbug: The Art of P. T. Barnum.* Boston: Little, Brown, 1973.

Hounshell, David. *From the American System to Mass Production, 1800–1932: The Development of Manufacturing Technology in the United States.* Baltimore: Johns Hopkins University Press, 1984.

Koehn, Nancy F. *Brand New: How Entrepreneurs Earned Consumers' Trust from Wedgwood to Dell.* Boston: Harvard Business School Press, 2001.

Strasser, Susan. *Waste and Want: A Social History of Trash.* New York: Metropolitan Books, 1999.

Railroads and mass distribution

Ambrose, Stephen E. *Nothing Like It in the World: The Men Who Built the Transcontinental Railroad, 1863–1869.* New York: Simon & Schuster, 2000.

Atherton, Lewis. *The Frontier Merchant in Mid-America.* St. Louis: University of Missouri Press, 1971.

Balleisen, Edward. *Fraud: An American History from Barnum to Madoff.* Princeton, NJ: Princeton University Press, 2017.

Cochran, Thomas C. *Railroad Leaders, 1845–1890: The Business Mind in Action.* Cambridge, MA: Harvard University Press, 1953.

Dunlavy, Colleen A. *Politics and Industrialization: Early Railroads in the United States and Prussia.* Princeton, NJ: Princeton University Press, 1994.

Mihm, Stephen. *A Nation of Counterfeiters: Capitalist, Con Men, and the Making of the United States.* Cambridge, MA: Harvard University Press, 2009.

Spears, Timothy B. *100 Years on the Road: The Traveling Salesman in American Culture.* New Haven, CT: Yale University Press, 1995.

Styles, T. J. *The First Tycoon: The Epic Life of Cornelius Vanderbilt.* New York: Alfred A. Knopf, 2009.

White, Richard. *Railroaded: The Transcontinentals and the Making of Modern America.* New York: W. W. Norton, 2011.

An industrial country

Cannadine, David. *Mellon: An American Life.* New York: Alfred A. Knopf, 2006.

Chernow, Ron. *Titan: The Life of John D. Rockefeller, Sr.* New York: Random House, 1998.

Cronon, William. *Nature's Metropolis: Chicago and the Great West.* New York: W. W. Norton, 1992.

Laird, Pamela. *Advertising Progress: American Business and the Rise of Consumer Marketing.* Baltimore: Johns Hopkins University Press, 1998.

Leach, William. *Land of Desire: Merchants, Power, and the Rise of a New American Culture.* New York: Pantheon Books, 1993.

Lears, T. J. Jackson. *Fables of Abundance: A Cultural History of Advertising in America.* New York: Basic Books, 1995.

Tedlow, Richard. *Giants of Enterprise: Seven Business Innovators and the Empires They Built.* New York: Harper Business, 2003.

Wilkins, Mira. *The Emergence of Multinational Enterprise: American Business Abroad from the Colonial Era to 1914.* Cambridge, MA: Harvard University Press, 1981.

Modern companies

Chandler, Alfred D. *Strategy and Structure: Chapters in the History of the American Industrial Enterprise.* Cambridge, MA: MIT Press, 1990. First published 1962.

Cortada, James. *Before the Computer: IBM, NCR, Burroughs, and Remington Rand and the Industry They Created, 1865–1956.* Princeton, NJ: Princeton University Press, 1993.

Clarke, Sally H. *Trust and Power: The Modern Corporation, and the Making of the United States Automobile Market.* New York: Cambridge University Press, 2007.

Drucker, Peter. *Management: Tasks, Responsibilities, Practices.* New York: Harper & Row, 1974.

Friedman, Walter A. *Fortune Tellers: The Story of America's First Economic Forecasters*. Princeton, NJ: Princeton University Press, 2013.

Henderson, Alexa Benson. *Atlanta Life Insurance: Guardians of Black Economic Dignity*. Tuscaloosa: University of Alabama Press, 1990.

John, Richard. *Network Nation: Inventing American Telecommunications*. Cambridge, MA: Harvard University Press, 2010.

Marchand, Roland. *Advertising the American Dream: Making Way for Modernity, 1920–1940*. Berkeley: University of California Press, 1986.

Pak, Susie J. *Gentlemen Bankers: The World of J. P. Morgan*. Cambridge, MA: Harvard University Press, 2014.

Strouse, Jean. *Morgan: American Financier*. New York: Random House, 2012.

Tedlow, Richard. *New and Improved: The Story of Mass Marketing in America*. Boston: Harvard Business School Press, 1996.

Walker, Juliet E. K. *The History of Black Business in America: Capitalism, Race, Entrepreneurship to 1865*. Chapel Hill: University of North Carolina Press, 2003.

Weare, Walter. *Black Business in the New South: A Social History of the North Carolina Mutual Life Insurance Company*. Chapel Hill: University of North Carolina Press, 1973. Reprinted 1993.

Further reading

Crisis and war

Badger, Anthony. *FDR: The First Hundred Days*. New York: Hill and Wang, 2008.

Field, Alex. *A Great Leap Forward: 1930s Depression U.S. Economic Growth*. New Haven, CT: Yale University Press, 2012.

Herman, Arthur. *Freedom's Forge: How American Business Produced the Victory in World War II*. New York: Random House, 2012.

Klein, Maury. *A Call to Arms: Mobilizing America for World War II*. New York: Bloomsbury Press, 2013.

Leuchtenburg, William E. *Franklin D. Roosevelt and the New Deal, 1932–1940*. New York: Harper Perennial, 2009.

McKenna, Christopher D. *The World's Newest Profession: Management Consulting in the Twentieth Century*. Cambridge: Cambridge University Press, 2006.

Phillips-Fein, Kim. *Invisible Hands: The Businessmen's Crusade against the New Deal*. New York: W. W. Norton, 2009.

Rhodes, Richard. *The Making of the Atomic Bomb*. New York: Simon & Schuster, 1988.

Wilson, Mark. *Destructive Creation: American Business and the Winning of World War II*. Philadelphia: University of Pennsylvania Press, 2016.

Corporate America

Brooks, John. *Business Adventures: Twelve Classic Tales from the World of Wall Street*. New York: Open Road, 1969.

Chandler, Alfred D. "The Competitive Performance of U.S. Industrial Enterprises since the Second World War." *Business History Review* 68, no. 1 (Spring 1994): 1–72.

Channon, Derek F. *The Services Industries: Strategy, Structure, and Financial Performance*. London: Macmillan, 1978.

Judt, Tony. *Postwar: A History of Europe since 1945*. New York: Penguin Press, 2005.

Kanter, Rosabeth Moss. *Men and Women of the Corporation*. New York: Basic Books, 1977.

Kwolek-Folland, Angel. *Incorporating Women: A History of Women and Business in the United States*. New York: Twayne, 1998.

Laird, Pamela Walker. *Pull: Networking and Success since Benjamin Franklin*. Cambridge, MA: Harvard University Press, 2006.

Mills, C. Wright. *White Collar: The American Middle Classes*. New York: Oxford University Press, 1951.

Whyte, William H. *The Organization Man*. New York: Simon & Schuster, 1956.

Yeager, Mary A., ed. *Women in Business*. Cheltenham, UK: Edward Elgar, 1999.

Entrepreneurs and the global economy

Berlin, Leslie. *The Man behind the Microchip: Robert Noyce and the Invention of Silicon Valley*. Oxford: Oxford University Press, 2005.

Berlin, Leslie. *Troublemakers: How a Generation of Silicon Valley Upstarts Invented the Future*. New York: Simon & Schuster, 2017.

Castells, Manuel. *The Internet Galaxy: Reflections on the Internet, Business, and Society*. Oxford: Oxford University Press, 2002.

Chandler, Alfred D. *Inventing the Electronic Century: The Epic Story of the Consumer Electronics and Computer Industry*. New York: Free Press, 2001.

Cheffins, Brian R. *The Public Company Transformed.* New York: Oxford, 2018.

Christensen, Clay. *The Innovator's Dilemma: The Revolutionary Book That Will Change the Way You Do Business.* New York: Collins Business Essentials, 2005.

Henderson, Rebecca. *Reimagining Capitalism: How Business Can Save the World.* New York: PublicAffairs, 2020.

Ho, Karen. *Liquidated: An Ethnography of Wall Street.* Durham, NC: Duke University Press, 2009.

Isaacson, Walter. *Steve Jobs.* New York: Simon & Schuster, 2011.

Khan, Lina. "Amazon's Antitrust Paradox." *The Yale Law Journal* 126, no. 3 (2017): 710–805.

McAfee, Andrew, and Erik Brynjolfsson. *Machine Platform Crowd: Harnessing Our Digital Future.* New York: W. W. Norton, 2017.

Rose, Mark H. *Market Rules: Bankers, Presidents, and the Origins of the Great Recession.* Philadelphia: University of Pennsylvania Press, 2018.

Saxenian, AnnaLee. *Regional Advantage: Culture and Competition in Silicon Valley and Route 128.* Cambridge, MA: Harvard University Press, 1996.

Stone, Brad. *The Everything Store: Jeff Bezos and the Age of Amazon.* New York: Back Bay Books, 2014.

Tedlow, Richard. *Andy Grove: The Life and Times of an American.* New York: Portfolio, 2006.

Tooze, Adam. *Crashed: How a Decade of Financial Crisis Changed the World.* New York: Viking Books, 2018.

Whittington, Richard. *Opening Strategy: Professional Strategists and Practice Change, 1960 to Today.* Oxford: Oxford University Press, 2019.

Zuboff, Shoshana. *The Age of Surveillance Capitalism: The Fight for a Human Future at the New Frontier of Power.* New York: PublicAffairs, 2019.

Index

Index